Water for Growth: California's New Frontier

• • •

Ellen Hanak

2005

Library of Congress Cataloging-in-Publication Data

Hanak, Ellen.

Water for growth : California's new frontier / Ellen Hanak.

p. cm.

Includes bibliographical references.

ISBN: 1-58213-108-2

1. Water-supply—California. 2. Water resources development—
California. I. Title.

HD1694.C2H25 2005

363.6'1'09794—dc22

2005015395

Foreword

Does California have enough water for future growth? The question is usually asked with an implied answer—No. Yet, for years it has been widely known that 80 percent of the water in California is used for agriculture—and often in highly inefficient ways. Some have even argued that we do not have a water shortage problem but a water allocation problem—a very different situation, but a challenge nonetheless.

So what is the answer to the question, "Is there enough water for future growth?" PPIC research fellow Ellen Hanak provides a very encouraging answer in this report.

First, ample opportunities are available over the coming decades to meet the state's needs through diverse approaches, including groundwater banking, recycling, improvements in urban water-use efficiency, and water transfers that can help supplement surface storage— the option that dominated California's water strategy in the early part of the last century.

Second, the author argues that on both the *demand* and *supply* side of the equation, future solutions are in the hands of local and regional agencies. After surveying city and county land-use planners, the author concludes that the "disconnect" between utilities and local governments is not as large as many might have imagined or feared. Six out of 10 land-use agencies participate in the planning activities of at least some of their local utilities, and nearly as many are active in water policy groups concerned with regional resource management. The survey also showed that over half of all cities and most counties—housing over half of the state's residents—have some form of local oversight policy to guard against the building of new residential developments without adequate water supply.

In sum, the author concludes that there are plenty of opportunities for balancing the supply and demand of water in the coming decades.

However, the state will have to play a role in creating the right incentives at the local level, and local and regional agencies will have to make sure that they are taking full advantage of the options available to them—conservation, storage, proper pricing, and thoughtful planning of new developments. Water supply and demand will always be a controversial subject. However, the author concludes that even as urban areas continue to expand, reasonable solutions to the efficient use of water will be well within reach.

David W. Lyon
President and CEO
Public Policy Institute of California

Summary

In California, rarely a week goes by without at least one local news article on a topic that looms large in the minds of policymakers and the public: Will we have enough water to support continued population growth? Although California's rate of growth has slowed since the 1970s and 1980s, the absolute increases predicted over the coming decades are indeed phenomenal. Between 2000 and 2030, the state is expected to add 14 million residents, to reach a total of 48 million.

The specter of a parched future stems in part from the recognition that much of the state's population lives in areas that rely on "imported" water—water brought in from distant north-state rivers, Sierra Nevada watersheds, or even beyond California's borders. It is also clear that the old way of doing business—damming up rivers and building aqueducts to move the captured surface water—is, in and of itself, no longer a viable strategy for accommodating growth. As the environmental costs of such projects have become apparent, the hurdles for approving new surface storage have become much higher. In response, water planners have begun considering alternative sources, such as groundwater banking, recycling, and desalination, as well as options to stretch existing supplies through water marketing and conservation. Arguably, water supply planning has become more complex as a result of this shift.

Although the California Department of Water Resources (DWR) periodically updates a statewide water plan, the frontline agencies responsible for meeting water supply needs are the hundreds of municipal utilities serving the state's residential and commercial customers. Key drivers of local water demand growth are also in local hands: City and county governments are responsible for approving land-use decisions—general and specific plans, zoning, and subdivision maps—that affect not only the quantity but also the footprint of local development. The footprint is important, because landscaping frequently accounts for more than half of all municipal water use.

The passage in 2001 of Senate Bill (SB) 610 and SB 221, the "show me the water" laws, can be considered a defining moment in California's development. These laws, similar to those being put in place across the American West, require the demonstration of adequate long-term water supplies before the approval of large development projects. This screening condition puts a spotlight on local land-use decisions that would have been inconceivable for most of the past century, when it was typically assumed that new supplies could be mobilized to accommodate new residents. In this sense, water has become the new frontier for growth in California.

This study examines how well California is faring in meeting the water supply challenges of growth. It begins with an assessment of trends in population and housing—both factors influencing demand—and an overview of the statewide portfolio of water supply options. The focus then shifts to the local level. First, the report examines the performance of water utilities in the most recently completed round of Urban Water Management Plans (UWMPs)—a state-mandated long-term water planning document required for all utilities serving at least 3,000 customers or delivering more than 3,000 acre-feet of water annually. Next, it draws on an original survey of local governments to see how they are integrating water supply concerns into land-use planning.

Big Picture Trends

If per capita urban water use were to remain at 2000 levels of 232 gallons per person per day, California would be facing an expansion of water demand by 40 percent, or 3.6 million acre-feet, by 2030. The "current trends" analysis in DWR's most recent California Water Plan Update (Bulletin 160-05) projects a slightly smaller increase (3.1 million acre-feet); this assumes that utilities continue to adopt the conservation measures they have already agreed to. However, projected trends in residential growth suggest that there may be upward pressures beyond this mark. Although new plumbing and appliance codes will moderate indoor use in new homes, growth patterns are likely to increase pressure on outdoor uses. Half of all new residents are expected to live in the state's three rapidly growing inland regions—the Inland Empire, the San

Joaquin Valley, and the Sacramento Metro region—where the harsher climate leads to higher use of water for landscaping needs. Single-family homes, which use more water outdoors, are also more common there.

Nevertheless, a review of supply options—drawing mainly on analysis from Bulletin 160-05—suggests that ample opportunities will be available over the coming decades. These options are diverse; groundwater banking, recycling, and water transfers are each likely to play at least as big a role as the expansion of surface storage. One of the largest "reservoirs" is urban conservation, which could make over 2 million acre-feet of new water available cost-effectively. Every new supply option faces at least some institutional hurdles, whether to gain public acceptance or to meet environmental approvals. But progress is being made on various fronts to overcome these hurdles.

Local Water Planning

Municipal utilities have come a long way since the mid-1980s, when the first Urban Water Management Plans were due. Long-term planning documents for 2000 were submitted by the vast majority of eligible agencies, serving over three-quarters of the state's population. However, our analysis revealed several weaknesses in the reporting system. One-sixth of eligible agencies submitted no plan whatsoever; a significant portion of submitted plans lacked detailed projections of supply and demand; and detailed series often deviated considerably from aggregate figures presented elsewhere in the plans. Finally, both now and in the future, a majority of utilities are reporting substantial normal-year surpluses. The magnitudes involved—some 2 million acre-feet per year—suggest that many utilities are banking on "paper water" already being used by someone else within the state's water system.

Integrating Water and Land Use

Our survey of city and county land-use planners suggests that the "disconnect" between utilities and local governments is not as big as many might have imagined or feared. Six out of 10 land-use agencies participate in the planning activities of at least some of their local utilities, and nearly as many are active in water policy groups concerned with regional resource management.

A central concern has been that the local government-utility disconnect will lead to the approval of new housing development without adequate water supplies, putting existing and new residents at risk of shortages. We find that over half of all cities and most counties, housing over half of the state's residents, have some form of local oversight policy to guard against this possibility.

SB 610 and SB 221 are nevertheless playing an important safety net function, catching projects that would otherwise fall through the cracks. Within the first three years, nearly 20 percent of local governments without their own water adequacy screening policies expected to conduct reviews under the new laws. Overall compliance with the laws appears good, and local governments are reviewing many projects smaller than those required by law (above 500 units).

This early implementation experience should assuage the worst fears on both sides of the water and growth debates. The new review process is not generating a flood of lawsuits against developers and water agencies. Nor is it systematically glossing over water supply problems to push ahead with new projects. In various places, developers are being sent back to the drawing board to come up with more secure supply options, and many projects are being designed to incorporate recycling and conservation.

The lawsuits that have been filed do tend to be linked to local controversies about the desirability of growth per se, not just to water supply. These controversies have nevertheless proven a useful testing ground for the enforceability of the state laws. Appellate court rulings have put developers, land-use authorities, and utilities on notice that both new housing development water supply assessments and UWMPs can be successfully challenged if they do not adequately analyze long-term supply reliability.

Meeting the Water Supply Challenges of Growth

Although success is far from guaranteed, these findings suggest that California is well positioned to tackle the challenges of finding and managing water for growth. Public discussions tend to focus on the more obvious risk of failure: chronic water shortages in areas without adequate supplies. But another, more hidden, risk concerns housing supply. If communities reject growth rather than finding water supply solutions compatible with it, the state faces the prospect of growing housing shortages.

To avoid either scenario, California's utilities and local governments face four key challenges: (1) strengthening long-term water planning, (2) streamlining water adequacy screening for new development, (3) realizing the potential of water conservation, and (4) consolidating progress in groundwater management.

Strengthening Long-Term Water Planning

Progress is needed to bring UWMPs to the level where they can serve as a basis for assessing long-term supply reliability. The stakes are now higher, because a well-documented UWMP can be used to demonstrate water availability for new development. The next round of UWMPs, due in December 2005, is an opportunity for progress.

The consistent message from the 2000-round is that plans are better when utilities are not working in isolation. This means making the most of existing utility networks and fostering new ones where these do not exist. It also means drawing in city and county land-use planners, whose involvement is key for water demand planning. Finally, plans are better when the utilities consult with the general public and local citizens' groups. An added benefit of this process is that utilities may thereby help allay public concerns about long-term supply reliability.

Streamlining Water Adequacy Reviews

Through a combination of local and state policies, the vast majority of California's local jurisdictions now screen for long-term water availability before approving new development. Given the lead times for mobilizing new supplies, this process can protect communities from the risk of chronic water shortages. The challenge is to screen well without unreasonably slowing housing growth. We estimate that since the mid-1990s, jurisdictions with screening policies have approved 13 to 22 percent fewer residential construction permits than jurisdictions without these policies. Several mechanisms are at work: longer delays before approval, downsizing or refusal of projects, and an increase in the climate of uncertainty surrounding the approval process.

Streamlining the review process can minimize these effects, without sacrificing rigor. To streamline, communities need to develop good long-term planning documents and to find efficient ways to pay for new supplies.

Equity considerations might weigh in favor of funding new supplies by raising water rates, a practice that would also encourage conservation. When residents resist such a move, explicit impact fees for new water may be a good alternative. Under this system, the utility, not the developer, undertakes responsibility to mobilize the new water. Water resources become part of the buy-in fee for development, along with such other public facilities as schools, roads, and water and wastewater treatment and delivery.

Such an approach, widely used in Colorado as well as Southern Nevada, should both reduce delays and remove much of the uncertainty from the approval process. A potential criticism of water resource impact fees is that they will raise the price of new housing. If impact fees allow more housing to be built, however, this criticism does not necessarily hold.

In this vision, streamlining reviews goes hand in hand with a policy to accommodate growth by making new water available. Growth itself is the real battleground in some communities, where activists have tried to block new water projects that would make room for new residents. More broadly, it is fair to wonder how many Californians view conservation as a legitimate way to accommodate growth. One telltale sign is the large number of communities that screen new development for water availability while failing to adopt conservation policies for existing residents.

Realizing the Potential of Water Conservation

In the years to come, California faces a twofold conservation challenge: curbing the water demands of new housing while convincing existing residents to cut back on their uses. The picture emerging from the 2000-round of UWMPs is not encouraging on either score: The plans anticipate constant per capita use to 2020, to be met with net increases in water supplies. The trends in water pricing are not particularly encouraging, either, with only limited progress in the adoption of tiered rate structures since the mid-1990s. Tiered rates are least prevalent in the fast-growing inland areas where this type of pricing could do the most to moderate use. In the San Joaquin Valley and the Sacramento Metro region, many homes still have no meters at all.

Politically, it may be easier to impose conservation on new development than on existing users. Getting existing residents to share the resource is more difficult because of the sense of entitlement that comes with existing water-rights law. As water becomes scarcer (and more expensive) statewide, there are no automatic levers to induce conservation in communities that choose not to conserve.

Although "soft" programs, such as public education, can play a role, it is likely that incentives will be needed to make substantial progress on this front. One option is to pay existing residents to conserve. This is the principle behind using state grants or impact fees to fund such programs as retrofits and turf replacement. An alternative, potentially complementary, path is to raise water fees. California water rates are still quite low in relation to median incomes. Tiered rate structures are a potentially powerful conservation tool, which also offer substantial equity benefits.

Consolidating Progress in Groundwater Management

Among the potential water sources to support growth, groundwater—fresh water found in underground aquifers—poses the greatest local management challenges. Unlike surface water, which is regulated by the state, groundwater is considered a local resource. Unsustainable pumping—commonly known as overdraft—is a problem in much of the San Joaquin Valley and in various other areas. It can lead to dry wells, land subsidence, and saltwater intrusion. Groundwater banking—using space made available by pumping—can augment usable water supplies considerably.

Groundwater is the largest single source of new supplies projected by the UWMPs, and two-thirds of the increase is projected in areas outside fully managed basins. In some of these areas, conflicts have already begun to emerge, as developers plan to use groundwater to supply new housing projects.

Managed basins—run either by a court-appointed water master or a special groundwater district—are able to resolve such conflicts. They have active monitoring systems and a well-established method for regulating use, either through explicit water rights or through prices. In unmanaged basins, good technical information is often lacking, and there are neither clear use-rights nor pump fees to help regulate withdrawals. Groundwater banking is also compromised when the rules are not clear.

Over the past decade, water users in many unmanaged areas have embarked on initiatives to improve basin oversight through voluntary schemes. Groundwater management plans and joint powers authorities have begun to improve the information base. In some cases, they have also made progress in supply management. As growth pressures increase, these systems will be put to the test. One question is whether voluntary models can lead to "friendly" adjudications, wherein users commit to apportioning use-rights in a nonadversarial process. The alternative to firmer operating rules is likely to be increasing overdraft, heightened risks of shortages, and costly, protracted legal battles.

How Can the State Help?

To date, the state's main role has been to facilitate better local water and land-use planning through enabling legislation, financial incentives, and technical support. Both the Urban Water Management Plan Act and the "show me the water" laws rely on citizen enforcement rather than on direct state oversight. Billions of dollars in state water bond funds have put the state in a position to reward local entities for taking positive actions. Legislation now makes state grants contingent on submission of a complete UWMP and prioritizes collaborative water management projects. DWR's technical support to urban water planning and water adequacy reviews has primarily consisted of outreach on how to comply with the law. For groundwater, DWR has become more involved in some regions, participating in management initiatives and assisting with basin investigations.

An alternative form of intervention is direct regulatory action. To date, such actions have focused on conservation. They include legislation requiring water-saving fixtures and appliances in new homes and a series of laws to prod municipal utilities to use meters. Significantly, the most recent meter bill, AB 2572, passed in 2004, introduces the possibility of withholding new water supply permits from noncomplying utilities. Recent comments from the State Water Resources Control Board, which oversees surface water rights, suggest that it is thinking along the same lines.

In our view, there is more room in California's future for regulatory actions backed by sticks rather than financial carrots. In particular, withholding permits is a potentially powerful tool to encourage local entities to manage water resources responsibly. Financial incentives, meanwhile, may not always be justified. They may also set a bad precedent if utilities (and local water users) come to expect taxpayer subsidies for projects that could be funded locally through water-related fees.

The time may also be at hand to solicit greater technical contributions from the state in the analysis of water supply reliability. Local oversight will remain essential to the UWMP process, but DWR could play a valuable role in helping to screen plan quality. Similarly, DWR can aid the local decisionmaking process on groundwater use for new development by serving as a neutral participant in basin analysis. Joint assessments involving DWR and locals can often provide the best opportunities for pooling available information to assess basin capacity.

Some of these policy shifts may not be popular with local entities, but they do not require a radical overhaul of the system of local control. Our analysis suggests that these shifts are more important than further refinements of local obligations under the UWMP Act or the water adequacy laws. In a few short years, the message of the water adequacy laws has gotten across. California now faces the task of promoting streamlined reviews and responsible local management of water resources. In this way, we can suitably recognize water's role as a frontier for growth, without letting that frontier become inhospitable.

Contents

Figures

Tables

Acknowledgments

This study would not have been possible without the generous assistance of the members of California's water and land-use planning communities. Over 300 city and county planning officials responded to our mail survey on water and growth issues, and many provided detailed follow-up information in phone interviews. The Department of Water Resources (DWR) made available its database on the 2000 Urban Water Management Plans, and numerous local water agency officials helped to clarify elements of their planning process with us. Maps of water agency service areas were graciously provided by the U.S. Bureau of Reclamation, DWR, the Association of Bay Area Governments, and various regional and local water agencies. Information on water rate structures and connection fees was made available by the Irvine, California, offices of the engineering consulting firm Black and Veatch. These contributions made it possible to provide a detailed, quantitative overview of how California's local water utilities and land-use planning departments are facing the challenges of growth.

In its early stages, the study benefited from guidance from a number of individuals closely involved in the process of linking water and land-use planning, including Randele Kanouse of the East Bay Municipal Utilities District; Mary Ann Dickinson and Katie Shulte Joung of the California Urban Water Conservation Council; David Smith and Tim Piasky of the Building Industry Association of Southern California; David Todd and Greg Smith of DWR; Jeff Loux of the University of California, Davis; Grace Chan, Brandon Goshi, and Warren Teitz of the Metropolitan Water District of Southern California; and Deborah Braver, independent consultant, formerly with the Water Conservation Office, DWR. During the course of the research, the study also benefited from regular contact with DWR's California Water Plan Update team, in particular Kamyar Guivetchi, Rich Juricich, and Scott Matyac.

At PPIC, Michael Teitz provided overall guidance on the research, and Paul Lewis provided helpful insights on the conduct of the mail survey. Two very capable research associates were involved in the project. Antonina Simeti, now a graduate student in City and Regional Planning at the Massachusetts Institute of Technology, developed the geographic information systems database on water utility service areas and oversaw the implementation of the survey of land-use planners. David Haskel handled various aspects of the subsequent work, including phone interviews with water and land-use officials and analysis of new water supply options.

In the final stages, very helpful reviews of the draft report were provided by Jaime Calleja Alderete (PPIC), David Groves (RAND Corporation), Michael Hanemann (University of California, Berkeley), Jon Haveman (PPIC), Rich Juricich, Randele Kanouse, Jeff Loux, Scott Matyac, David Todd, and Michael Teitz. Gary Bjork (PPIC) and Patricia Bedrosian (RAND Corporation) provided editorial assistance.

Although the responsibility for conclusions drawn in this report rests entirely with the author, the contributions of all those who helped at various stages were invaluable and greatly appreciated.

Acronyms

AB	Assembly Bill
APFO	Adequate Public Facilities Ordinance
BMP	Best Management Practice
CALFED	State and federal program for the San Francisco–San Joaquin Bay Delta
CEQA	California Environmental Quality Act
CLWA	Castaic Lake Water Agency
COG	Council of Governments
CUWCC	California Urban Water Conservation Council
CVP	Central Valley Project
CVPIA	Central Valley Project Improvement Act
DMM	Demand Management Measure
DOF	Department of Finance
DWR	Department of Water Resources
EBMUD	East Bay Municipal Utilities District
EIR	Environmental Impact Review
EPA	Environmental Protection Agency
gpcd	Gallons per capita per day
IBR	Increasing Block Rate
KCWA	Kern County Water Agency
LAFCO	Local Agency Formation Commission
MSA	Metropolitan Statistical Area
MWDSC	Metropolitan Water District of Southern California
OFHEO	Office of Federal Housing Enterprise Oversight
OPR	Office of Planning and Research
SB	Senate Bill
SCAG	Southern California Association of Governments
SCVWD	Santa Clara Valley Water District
SFPUC	San Francisco Public Utilities Commission
SNWA	Southern Nevada Water Authority

SWP	State Water Project
UWMP	Urban Water Management Plan
USBR	United States Bureau of Reclamation

1. Water for Growth: The New Frontier

Finding enough water to support population growth has become a key resource management challenge for California and other western states. Historically, the region's development was predicated on harnessing water through the construction of large-scale dams, reservoirs, and conveyance systems. However, over the past 25 years, water supply systems have come under increasing stress. The model of building more dams to accommodate growth has been seriously challenged on environmental and financial grounds. Supplies available for human use have actually been cut back in many places, following court or legislative determinations that existing projects have taken too much water away from the environment.

Meanwhile, population is increasing rapidly. Although rates of growth are higher in some of the smaller western states, the absolute increases are largest in California. California's population grew by over 10 million people between 1980 and 2000 and is expected to increase by another 14 million by 2030, to reach a total of 48 million (Department of Finance, 2004). With each new household comes additional demand for residential water.

Given the obstacles to constructing large new surface storage projects, policymakers and planners have been considering a portfolio of alternatives for bringing supply and demand into balance over the years ahead. Options include expansion of nontraditional sources of supply (e.g., underground storage, recycling, and desalination), reallocation through water marketing, and conservation. Although each of these options offers advantages, none are entirely straightforward to implement. Underground storage and reallocation through the market are both potentially low-cost alternatives, but each faces significant institutional hurdles. Expansion of recycled water use requires modifications in plumbing systems and, more important, in the way residential users think about reusing treated wastewater. Desalination is becoming more plausible, but it is still a relatively high-cost source. Finally, although the benefits of conservation are readily apparent, this option can be costly in terms of both the technological investments needed to enable the savings and the consequences for "quality of life" if it entails restrictions on landscaping, which can account for over half of residential water use.

Decentralized Water and Land-Use Planning

The need to weigh alternatives, mobilize investment resources, and overcome institutional barriers to putting in place a diversified water supply portfolio has made the task of water supply planning more complex than in the era of large surface storage projects. Meanwhile, the focus of the planning effort has shifted from the state to the local level. Whereas many large water projects of the past were undertaken with state and federal leadership, most current options are local or regional in scope, falling under the responsibility of municipal water utilities. The Department of Water Resources (DWR) produces a statewide water plan every five years or so, but this document is too general to provide local agencies with concrete planning assistance.

The institutional landscape of California's water utilities is a study in diversity, with hundreds of agencies differing in size and structure. The largest municipal wholesale supplier, the Metropolitan Water District of Southern California (MWDSC), now serves 17 million residents, easily a thousand times more than some of the smaller utilities. Some retail agencies—those that directly deliver water to homes and businesses—are part of a network of a large wholesale supplier, such as MWDSC, whereas others are independent. Utilities may be constituted as special districts, municipal departments, or private companies.

Although utilities are free to engage in other water planning activities, the roughly 400 largest wholesale and retail municipal suppliers (those with at least 3,000 connections or delivering at least 3,000 acre-feet per year) are required by the Urban Management Water Plan Act to prepare 20-year Urban Water Management Plans (UWMPs) every five years. This law was introduced in 1983 and has been strengthened in several revisions. Utilities must submit copies of the plans to DWR, but the department has no authority to evaluate their quality. The only sanction, introduced in 2002, is that agencies whose reports are not "complete" (i.e., they do not cover all required topics) are not eligible for certain types of state financial support. This incentive may have some pull, because the state has recently had considerable financial resources to offer to local projects, thanks to the passage of several environmental bonds since 2000.

In roughly half of California's cities and in most counties, water supply planning is further complicated by the fact that water utilities and general-purpose governments operate as separate entities, whose physical boundaries only partly overlap. City and county governments are responsible for land-use decisions—general and specific plans, subdivision approval, and zoning—which critically affect community water demands. By the early 1990s, concerns over the water demand consequences of some large housing developments led the East Bay Municipal Utilities District (EBMUD), a large Bay Area supplier, to push for requirements that land-use authorities link their activities to the water planning process.

Over objections by associations representing cities and builders, Senate Bill (SB) 901 was passed in 1995, requiring that local governments conduct water supply assessments during the environmental reviews for large projects (above 500 units). In 2001, SB 610 strengthened these review requirements, and SB 221 made written verification of long-term water supply a precondition of final subdivision map approval. As with the Urban Water Management Plan Act, these laws rely largely on citizen enforcement by allowing the public to legally challenge a utility or local government that does not comply. The state's role has been limited to outreach on the scope of the laws and the means of compliance.

Linking Water and Land Use: The Policy Debates

Proponents of the new legislation have argued that it is a matter of common sense to ensure that local planning entities coordinate their efforts. Nevertheless, the "show me the water" laws continue to be the subject of considerable debate. Some critics have raised concerns that the review thresholds are too high—allowing many new projects to progress without scrutiny, despite their potential effect on local water availability. (Initially, SB 221 had proposed a review threshold of 200 homes, but this was revised upward in negotiations with cities and the building industry.) In this vein, there has already been a push for further legislation requiring that cities and counties include water elements in their general plans.

Meanwhile, others are wary that the new statutes may serve as a tool for antigrowth advocates, unreasonably blocking new housing in a state that already has a housing shortage. Many of the interest groups involved in the negotiations believe that there should be a five-year cooling-off period before any new state legislation is introduced in this area.

Recent public discussions have placed less emphasis on the local policy context. Under California law, cities and counties are free to establish their own water adequacy policies. Although it is well known that coastal communities in Santa Barbara and Marin Counties have long had strict policies linking water and housing, much less is known about how local governments across the state deal with these questions. Indeed, the debates on the pros and cons of the state laws are based on a presumption that local activity is very limited.

There is, similarly, surprisingly little discussion of the underlying premise of California's water planning system, which places ultimate responsibility with the local utilities. Yet it is the performance of these utilities, in conjunction with local land-use agencies, that will determine how well the state meets the water supply challenges of growth. Failure could be measured in two ways: on the one hand, if communities are put at risk of chronic shortfalls because of inadequate supply planning and, on the other, if water concerns lead communities to reject new housing rather than to find supply solutions that are compatible with accommodating the state's new residents.

Meeting the Water Supply Challenges of Growth

This study examines the dynamics of water supply and population growth in California, with a focus on local water and land-use planning mechanisms. Drawing on a range of data sources, including original surveys, the analysis explores the following questions: Which types of water utilities are demonstrating a capacity to plan for growth? Do the supply strategies they favor reflect realistic assumptions? How good are the lines of communication between land-use authorities and water utilities? How many local governments have their own procedures for reviewing the water supply implications of new development? Are the new "show me the water" laws encouraging better linkages? Are water adequacy policies slowing housing growth?

Chapter 2 begins with an overview of the water demand drivers in different parts of the state and the advantages and drawbacks of various supply options. The study then turns to a detailed analysis of the performance of local utilities and land-use planning authorities. Chapter 3 looks at utility water planning, with a focus on the latest round of Urban Water Management Plans, submitted between late 2000 and mid-2003. Drawing on a unique dataset developed for this study, it assesses the quality of the plans and analyzes the role of utility and community characteristics in plan performance. Chapter 4 shifts the focus to land-use agencies, presenting the results of a new survey of city and county planners on water and growth issues. It details the extent of their involvement in water planning, the prevalence of local water adequacy policies, and the experience to date with the new state laws linking water and land use.

The study then addresses the question at the heart of the policy debates on water and land-use legislation: Is water policy affecting housing growth? If communities are truly resource-constrained, slowing growth in line with water availability may be an appropriate outcome. As with any regulatory process, there are also risks of overcorrection, however. The most obvious risk is that antigrowth advocates may use the requirements as a pretext for limiting growth, irrespective of water supply conditions. A more nuanced version of this problem arises if communities choose to maintain high levels of per household water availability (and low water prices) rather than to make room for new residents through conservation. Chapter 5 explores these issues by analyzing the evidence to date from implementation of both state and local water adequacy policies.

Chapter 6 concludes by assessing the policy issues that face state and local entities in meeting the water supply challenges of growth. What mix of state, regional, and local policies can help California's communities in this quest? Should state oversight of local plans be augmented? Is there a need for greater institutional support for agencies with weaker planning capacity? What can local agencies do to streamline the approval process for new development while maintaining good stewardship of water resources? What is the appropriate role for carrots and sticks to encourage better local performance?

2. Water Demand Drivers and Supply Sources

Historically, much of California's water supply was developed to support the agriculture economy—the nation's largest. Despite decades of rapid population growth, municipal demand still accounts for a relatively small share of total water use, about four times less than that of the farm sector. But whereas agricultural demands are not increasing—and indeed are likely to decline as farmland is converted to residential uses—municipal demands are clearly on the rise.

So, too, are environmental water demands. Since the late 1980s, a series of court rulings, administrative decisions, and legislative actions have prompted the return of some developed water sources to instream flows and wildlife habitats. Although farmers, as the largest water users, have felt the brunt of these cutbacks, some urban users have also been affected. For instance, the city of Los Angeles has had to significantly reduce its use of southern Sierra Nevada water because excessive water diversions were destroying the ecosystem in Mono Lake and worsening the air quality in the Owens Valley. Overall, water users estimate that roughly 2 million acre-feet have been returned to environmental flows as a result of decisions affecting the San Francisco–San Joaquin Bay Delta and the Owens Valley region. The latest update of the California Water Plan, which uses estimates provided by the environmental community, reports that another 1 million acre-feet would be needed for some unmet environmental objectives. To prevent future problems, new water projects must now meet strict standards of environmental review.

The pressures facing water utilities will differ considerably across the state, depending on each region's population growth, climate, and the ease with which new supply sources can be mobilized. This chapter provides an overview of the demand drivers in light of recent and projected patterns of regional growth. It then considers the portfolio of potential new supplies.

Regional Population Trends

The regional categories used here and throughout the report group counties into seven geographic blocks (Figure 2.1). Two coastal regions—the Southern Coast and the San Francisco Bay Area—are the state's major metropolitan areas (Table 2.1). The less populated Central Coast region lies between them. Three inland regions—the Sacramento Metro region, the San Joaquin Valley, and the Inland Empire (Riverside and San Bernardino Counties)—have become the state's most rapidly growing areas. Rural counties with low populations and more limited growth pressure are grouped into a seventh category. Although there is a great deal of overlap, these regions differ somewhat from the 10 hydrologic regions DWR uses in its statewide planning exercises (Appendix Figure A.2). Because many of the hydrologic boundaries do not correspond to administrative boundaries, the hydrologic regions do not readily lend themselves to analysis of local government decisionmaking.

Both coastal metropolitan regions and the Inland Empire rely heavily on supplies imported from watersheds in the north and east of the state; the two southern regions also draw on the Colorado River. The Sacramento Metro region is relatively rich in surface and groundwater supplies, although growth has put pressure on both sources in some areas. The San Joaquin Valley—California's primary agricultural region—depends on imported surface water from the north and the east to bolster overtaxed groundwater basins. The Central Coast distinguishes itself by long-standing concerns over water supply issues, given its limited access to imported water. Water supply sources and conditions differ considerably across the rural counties.

For those concerned with the potential negative consequences of rapid population growth, the most recent projections from the Department of Finance (DOF), released in May 2004, provide some good news. Recent declines in fertility rates have led to a downward revision of growth rates. DOF now projects a statewide population of roughly 48 million by 2030, nearly 4 million less than the level projected

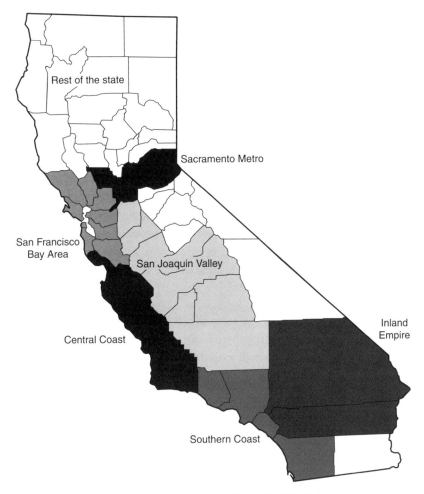

Rest of the state

Sacramento Metro

San Francisco
Bay Area

San Joaquin Valley

Inland
Empire

Central Coast

Southern Coast

NOTE: For a list of counties in each region, see Appendix Table A.1.

Figure 2.1—California's Regions

several years earlier.[1] The increase is nevertheless substantial, with over 14 million new residents between 2000 and 2030, or nearly 480,000 residents per year.

_____

[1]For a discussion of these trends and alternative population scenarios, see Johnson (2005). The previous projections were released in 1998.

Table 2.1

Regional Population Growth

Region	Average Annual Population Growth, 1990–2004 (%)	2004 Population	Projected Absolute Increase, 2004–2030
San Francisco Bay Area	1.1	7,009,400	2,167,215
Central Coast	1.2	1,411,700	322,941
Southern Coast	1.2	16,939,900	2,950,595
Inland Empire	2.6	3,663,200	2,279,518
San Joaquin Valley	2.1	3,615,600	2,303,055
Sacramento Metro	2.2	1,980,100	1,428,225
Rest of the state	1.4	1,524,050	515,172
California	1.4	36,143,950	11,966,721

SOURCE: Author's calculations using data from the Department of Finance (2004).

Although the Bay Area and especially the Southern Coast counties will continue to absorb a large share of this growth, the three inland regions will become increasingly populated, accounting for half of the total. By 2030, they will house nearly one-third of the state's residents. Indeed, the pull of cheaper housing is a contributing factor in this shift. In 2002, the median home price in the Inland Empire was $176,000, nearly half the price of homes in the neighboring coastal areas. This ratio was even more favorable for homes in the northern San Joaquin Valley counties of Stanislaus, San Joaquin, and Merced, relative to their Bay Area neighbors.

Water Demand Drivers

How this growth affects water demand will depend in part on structural factors. Per capita residential use differs considerably, depending on the type of indoor plumbing and two factors related to landscaping needs: climate and lot size. Water-use efficiency within new homes has generally improved as a result of changes in plumbing codes since the 1980s—notably, requirements to install low-flow showerheads and toilets. Beginning in 2007, all new washing machines sold in California will have to meet commercial water efficiency standards.

Housing Trends Will Put Pressure on Outdoor Use

The regional population trends may be more problematic with respect to outdoor uses, however. More extreme inland climates generate higher seasonal watering demands than the areas along the temperate coast.[2] In the interior valleys, landscape irrigation accounts for over half of residential use, versus less than one-third in coastal zones. Outdoor use also increases with lot size. People living in single-family homes, which have larger lots, use more water than those living in multifamily dwellings.[3]

In 2000, the two metropolitan coastal regions already had significantly higher shares of multifamily units than the inland areas (Figure 2.2). DWR estimates that in that year, per capita residential use in coastal regions ranged from 97 to 132 gallons per day, versus 177 to 337 gallons in the inland valleys (Appendix Table A.2).

If the recent past is an accurate guide, construction trends will reinforce the pressure on outdoor water use, because construction of single-family homes is on the rise in all regions except the Bay Area and the Southern Coast. Statewide, multifamily units have accounted for only 28 percent of new residential construction since 2000, versus 31 percent of the 2000 housing stock. One mitigating factor is the apparent decline in single-family lot sizes in recent decades.[4] Nevertheless, these trends suggest that measures to promote conservation will become increasingly important, not only to free up supplies from existing users but also to guard against the tendency for water use to rise in new homes with higher landscaping demands.

---

[2]See Department of Water Resources (1994) and Mayer et al. (1999).

[3]A study in MWDSC's service area found that per capita outdoor use for single-family home residents was twice as high as for those in multifamily units (Planning and Management Consultants, Ltd., 1991).

[4]In Riverside and Sacramento Counties, for instance, median lot sizes fell by about 1,000 square feet between the late 1970s and the late 1990s (author's calculations using county assessor records from DataQuick).

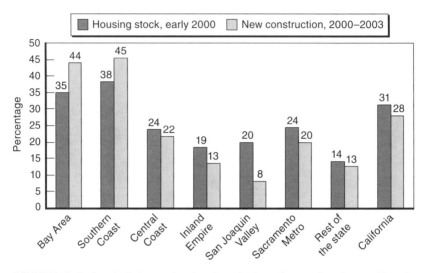

SOURCE: Author's calculations using data from the 2000 Census (housing stock) and the Construction Industry Research Board (new construction).

Figure 2.2—Share of Multifamily Homes in Housing Stock and in New Construction

Considerable Scope for Price-Based Incentives to Conserve

Utilities use a combination of price and nonprice measures to encourage conservation. Nonprice measures include "soft" programs, such as public education, and "hard" programs, such as regulatory requirements to use low-flow plumbing fixtures and appliances. Price measures include increasing the direct charges for water use as well as providing rebates to those who switch to more water-efficient technologies. Both types of conservation tools have been promoted actively since the early 1990s, when the state was reeling from a multiyear drought.

The California Urban Water Conservation Council (CUWCC), a voluntary association of water utilities formed in 1991, is at the center of this movement. It promotes and tracks the adoption of 14 Best Management Practices (BMPs). Two of these directly concern water rates: the adoption of metering (BMP 4) and of conservation pricing (BMP 11).

Metering is an issue because many communities in the Sacramento and San Joaquin Valleys have traditionally charged flat fees for water, regardless of the volume of use. There is considerable evidence that volumetric charges induce conservation.[5] A frequently cited comparison is that between the city of Clovis, which uses meters, and the neighboring city of Fresno, which does not. Per capita use in Clovis is roughly 40 percent lower (*Fresno Bee*, 2004). On average, the CUWCC estimates that meters reduce water use by about 20 percent.

State and federal policies have actively promoted the introduction of metering, but not without opposition. A 1991 state law (SB 229) requires that all new homes have meters but, significantly, it does not require that utilities read them or bill at the metered rate. The 1992 Central Valley Project Improvement Act (CVPIA) obliges all municipal contractors of the federally run Central Valley Project (CVP) to switch over to meters as a condition of contract renewal. Foot-dragging prompted the state legislature to pass Assembly Bill (AB) 514 in 2003, setting 2013 as a final deadline for compliance by CVP contractors. In 2004, after much back and forth, the legislature passed AB 2572, calling for all utilities with 3,000 or more customers to install meters over the next two decades and to begin using meters for billing by 2010 when these are available. AB 306, the earlier version of this bill introduced the year before, would have required metered pricing by 2009. It did not make it out of the assembly.

The loopholes and the acrimonious debates on introducing stricter legislation reflect the considerable local resistance to metering in some communities. This resistance has hinged on a variety of arguments. The cost of installing meters is said to outweigh the savings. There is also a perception that there is ultimately no water "wasted" in these areas because the excess is either recharged into the groundwater basin or, once treated, returned to streams. In at least one case, discussed below, objections to metering hinged on the concern that the conserved water would become available for unwanted new growth.

---

[5]See Hanemann and Hewitt (1995), Baumann, Boland, and Hanemann (1997), and Michelsen, McGuckin, and Stumpf (1999).

Under the current language of BMP 11, metering at uniform rates, which charge the same amount for each gallon used, is one form of conservation pricing, because it provides incentives for customers to reduce average levels of use. However, discussions are under way to revise the definition of this BMP, so that utilities would be required to regularly review the feasibility of moving to more aggressively conservation-oriented rate structures. Foremost among these is increasing block rate (IBR), or tiered, pricing, which charges higher rates for higher levels of use. A less common alternative, sometimes practiced in combination with IBRs, is seasonal pricing, under which rates are increased during the hot summer months of peak demand. IBRs are particularly attractive, because they seek to balance the incentive effects of higher water rates with their potentially negative distributional consequences. In general, water use increases with income, because higher-income households have larger lots and more water-using appliances. Tiered rates keep water for basic uses most affordable while encouraging conservation above those levels (for instance, for outdoor uses). By the estimates of one utility—the Irvine Ranch Water District in Orange County—an IBR policy combined with outreach reduced use by 12 percent (Gleick et al., 2003). Recent research suggests that consumers' sensitivity to water price changes rises considerably under IBR systems, making this a very important policy tool for conservation (Cavanagh, Hanemann, and Stavins, 2002; Dalhuisen et al., 2003). Industry analysts stress additional benefits from reduced operating and development costs (Chesnutt and Beecher, 1998).

The early 1990s drought prompted a marked shift from uniform rate structures toward increasing block rate pricing (Figure 2.3). Since the mid-1990s, however, there has been little further movement and, indeed, occasional backsliding to uniform rates. Progress away from nonmetered rate structures has been very limited and more recent. A handful of utilities still engage in the *reverse* of conservation pricing by providing quantity discounts for higher volumes of use with declining block rates.

Because some of the largest utilities have adopted increasing block rates, roughly half of the state's population now faces this type of conservation pricing (Table 2.2), versus only 7 percent without meters and 1 percent with declining rates. However, within the Sacramento

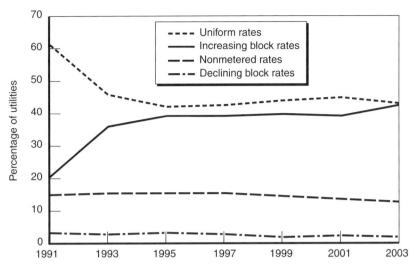

SOURCE: Author's calculations using survey data from Black and Veatch (1991–2003).
NOTE: The chart reports the share of utilities with each rate structure (total = 100%), using data from 214 utilities present in the survey in all years.

Figure 2.3—Utility Rate Structures in California, 1991–2003

Table 2.2

Percentage Distribution of Rate Structures Across the Population, 2003

	Declining	Nonmetered	Uniform	Increasing
Bay Area	0	1	57	42
Central Coast	3	0	40	57
Southern Coast	0	0	36	64
Inland Empire	0	0	57	43
San Joaquin Valley	6	55	25	13
Sacramento Metro	0	35	40	25
Rest of the state	2	10	65	22
California	1	7	43	50

SOURCE: Author's calculations using utility survey data from Black and Veatch (2003).

NOTES: Some rows do not sum to 100 because of rounding. The sample includes 384 utilities. The sample population covers 88 percent of the statewide total in that year. Coverage was lowest in the San Joaquin Valley (63%) and counties in the rest of the state (49%). Nine utilities with increasing block rates also use higher summer rates, as do three utilities with uniform rates.

Metro region and especially the San Joaquin Valley, nonmetered communities are still prevalent, and tiered pricing is quite limited. There is also a large margin for improvement in the Inland Empire, where over half of the residents still face uniform rates. These patterns suggest yet another reason for upward pressure on water demand in these fast-growing regions, and they highlight the importance of the legislature's recent success at pinning utilities down to a schedule for the adoption of metering.

Water Rates Are Still Low in California

Average water bills may be somewhat higher in California than in neighboring western states.[6] However, by the common metric of affordability—the share of median household income represented by the water bill—it appears that most California communities have a considerable margin for rate increases before water rates become burdensome. In 2003, only 3 percent of communities (covering 2% of the sampled population) had charges greater than 1.5 percent of median income, the cutoff for eligibility under special assistance programs (Table 2.3).[7] Another 12 percent of utilities (8% of the sampled population) had fees exceeding 1 percent of median income. Regions where water rates are relatively high—including the Central Coast and some north coast and mountain communities within the "rest of the state" category—appear more vulnerable than fast-growing Central Valley communities, where water rates are generally quite low.

---

[6]Using data from a 1996 utility survey by the American Water Works Association, we estimated average population-weighted annual bills of $284 for 119 California utilities, versus $233 for 90 utilities in eight other semi-arid western states (Arizona, Colorado, Nevada, New Mexico, Oklahoma, Texas, Utah, and Wyoming). We found a higher gap using data from the Environmental Protection Agency's (EPA's) 2000 Community Water System Survey ($438 for 107 California utilities versus $326 for 141 utilities in the eight other western states). Average bills for California from the EPA survey appear too high, however. As reported in Table 2.3, a more extensive statewide survey in 2003 finds an average bill of only $363.

[7]Specifically, the Safe Drinking Water State Revolving Fund, co-financed by federal and state authorities, gives priority grants and zero-interest loans to low-income communities (median household income below 65% of the statewide average) with water fees above this threshold. For other communities, the state considers charges of 2 percent of median household income to be potentially burdensome.

Table 2.3

Water Charges as a Share of Median Household Income, 2003

	No. of Communities in Sample	Average Yearly Water Bill ($)	Water Bill as % of Median Household Income	% with a Water Bill > 1% of Median Income	% with a Water Bill > 1.5% of Median Income
Bay Area	109	444	0.6	5	0
Southern Coast	176	385	0.7	13	1
Central Coast	38	457	0.9	29	11
Inland Empire	60	322	0.7	17	8
San Joaquin Valley	55	207	0.5	5	0
Sacramento Metro	34	248	0.5	3	0
Rest of the state	64	344	1.0	41	8
California	536	363	0.7	15	3

SOURCES: Author's calculations using water charges from Black and Veatch (2003) and median household income from the 2000 Census, adjusted for inflation with the Consumer Price Index for Urban Areas.

NOTES: "Communities" are defined as a pairing between a utility and a local jurisdiction (city or unincorporated area of a county). For jurisdictions with multiple utilities, the analysis assumes that the distribution of household income is the same across utility service areas. Population-weighted average bills are very close to the unweighted values presented here.

Projected Trends in Total Urban Use

Residential use is the largest component of urban water demand, accounting for over 60 percent of the total in recent years (Table 2.4). Other key components include commercial uses (businesses and institutions, such as schools and hospitals), large landscaping (golf courses, cemeteries, and parks), and industry. Commercial and large landscaping uses can be expected to mirror the demand growth for residential water, with population as a primary driver. Industry, which accounts for a relatively small share of urban use (6–7%), is less likely to grow commensurately. Over the coming decades, the structure of the economy is expected to move away from manufacturing and toward services, which are less water-intensive (Neumark, 2005).

Statewide, per capita urban use in a normal rainfall year—typified by the year 2000—is now roughly 232 gallons per capita per day (Table

2.4). Although that level would drop considerably during a multiyear drought, when strict outdoor watering restrictions apply, it barely fell in 2001, a single dry year, when only limited restrictions were in place. In drier years, the unrestricted demand for landscape watering tends to increase because rainfall does less of the job; the reverse is true in wet years.

If per capita use were to remain constant between 2000 and 2030 and population followed the trends projected by the Department of Finance (2004), demand would grow by 3.6 million acre-feet, a roughly 40 percent increase over current levels. Growth patterns are likely to push in the direction of higher outdoor water use, even as new plumbing and appliance codes moderate indoor use. The net effect on per capita use will depend, in part, on the extent to which utilities employ price and nonprice conservation policies.

Table 2.4

Statewide Urban Water Use

	Wet Year, 1998	Normal Year, 2000	Dry Year, 2001
Total annual use (millions of acre-feet)			
Residential	4.9	5.6	5.4
Outdoor portion	*2.0*	*2.3*	*2.3*
Commercial	1.3	1.6	1.6
Large landscapes	0.6	0.7	0.6
Industrial	0.5	0.6	0.6
Energy production	0.1	0.1	0.1
Losses and recharge	0.4	0.3	0.2
All urban[a]	7.8	8.9	8.6
Per capita use (gallons per day)			
All urban	213	232	223
Urban, excluding industrial	200	218	207
Residential	134	147	140

SOURCES: Department of Water Resources (2005). Per capita use is calculated using midyear population figures from the Department of Finance.

[a]The discrepancy between 2001 urban total use and its components is due to rounding.

In the California Water Plan's "current trends" scenario for water demand, average use is projected to fall to 221 gallons per capita per day (gpcd) by 2030 (–4.6%) if utilities simply continue to implement programs to which they have already agreed, and population, economic growth, and water-use patterns evolve as expected.[8] This would bring total new urban water demands down to 3.1 million acre-feet, somewhat less than the current water-use levels scenario (Figure 2.4). As will be seen below, some analysts estimate that a great deal more could be saved cost-effectively with the adoption of new conservation programs.

Two other water plan scenarios highlight the role of development patterns on demand pressures. The less resource-intensive scenario in Figure 2.4 allows for denser land use and greater responsiveness to water prices, resulting in a net water demand growth of only 1.5 million acre-

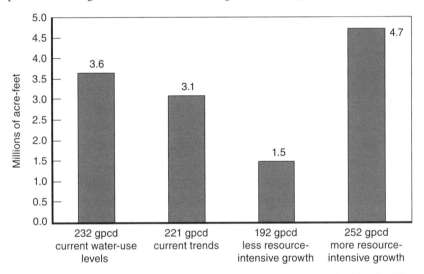

SOURCE: Author's calculations using data from Groves, Matyac, and Hawkins (2005).

Figure 2.4—Projected Urban Demand Growth, 2000–2030

---

[8]The demand analysis for the *California Water Plan Update* derives from Groves, Matyac, and Hawkins (2005).

feet.[9] Alternatively, the more resource-intensive scenario, with a more pronounced population shift toward hotter areas and single-family homes and less price responsiveness, would raise per capita use and bring new urban demands to 4.7 million acre-feet.[10] These scenarios underscore the importance of factoring in concerns about land use and the set of incentives facing residents and businesses when assessing the potential trajectory of water demand, both statewide and locally.

Other Pressures on Net Demands

In some places, utilities will need to locate new supply sources simply to meet existing demand. As part of its interstate obligations, California is now cutting back on its use of Colorado River water by 0.8 million acre-feet—surplus water previously used by Southern California urban utilities. Although these utilities are making up some of the difference through long-term transfers from agricultural contractors on the Colorado River, there is still a net gap that must be filled from other sources. Environmental concerns are also leading to further cutbacks for some urban utilities, including the city of Los Angeles (continued mitigation of the dry Owens Lake bed) and a private water supplier in the Monterey Peninsula (reduction of diversions from the Carmel River).

Additionally, some agencies may need to reduce groundwater use because of overdraft—the pumping of water in excess of recharge. DWR estimates that annual overdraft, which can cause problems ranging from higher pumping costs, to salinity, to falling land levels (or subsidence), is in the range of 1 million to 2 million acre-feet statewide. In some managed aquifers, such as the Mojave Basin, agencies have committed to reduce their withdrawals gradually to achieve sustainable yield. In many

---

[9]This scenario includes an 8.5 percent increase in the share of multifamily homes between 2000 and 2030; 6.5 and 8.3 percent increases, respectively, in single-family and multifamily household sizes; higher rates of conservation; and greater sensitivity to water prices by residences and businesses than in the current trends scenario.

[10]This scenario includes a 6.6 percent decrease in the share of multifamily homes; more rapid growth in the southern and inland regions; lower rates of conservation; and lower price sensitivity than in the current trends scenario. In the Water Plan's exercise, this scenario also allows for additional population growth, which we have netted out here to highlight the role of development patterns. All three scenarios assume a base increase in water use efficiency of 5 percent and a 20 percent increase in water prices.

parts of the state, groundwater management is still in its infancy, and users have not yet worked out systems for assigning responsibility for overdraft reduction. Contamination of groundwater basins—from chemicals such as MTBE and perchlorate—is also reducing the availability of groundwater in some areas; in others, expensive treatment methods are significantly adding to costs.

Supply Sources

For utilities facing demand increases or needing to compensate for supply reductions, solutions will differ depending on local opportunities and the extent of existing water rights. Some communities already hold rights or contracts to draw on considerably more water than they currently use. For agricultural or mining interests, unused rights would be considered nothing more than "paper water," under the "use-it-or-lose-it" principle of appropriative water-rights law. However, there is a legal tradition in California and elsewhere in the West of greater tolerance for municipal users to hold onto unused water rights in anticipation of future growth (Tarlock, 2001).

Fewer communities enjoy surplus water rights *and* the capacity to use them, via adequate conveyance and storage facilities. Construction of expanded capacity is thus a major focus in some places, through new conveyance projects and new surface and underground storage. Such projects also provide agencies with the opportunity to make use of water acquired through temporary or long-term transfers of water rights from other agencies. For agencies with insufficient water rights, other new sources include recycling, desalination of ocean water and brackish groundwater, and conservation.

One focus of the most recent California Water Plan Update has been to spotlight how much new water could be mobilized between now and 2030 from these various sources. The most recent estimates, which draw on assorted studies, indicate scope for expansion well above the range of expected growth in urban and environmental demand (Figure 2.5). The three largest categories, each potentially generating well over 1 million acre-feet, include urban use efficiency, groundwater storage, and recycling of municipal wastewater. New surface storage under state and federal sponsorship is expected to generate no more than 1 million acre-

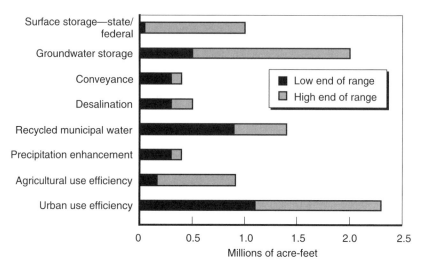

SOURCE: Department of Water Resources (2005).

Figure 2.5—Annual Production Potential from New Supply Sources and Conservation, 2000–2030

feet and improvements in agricultural use efficiency up to 0.9 million. A host of other strategies—including desalination, rainfall enhancement, and improvements in conveyance facilities and operations—are more limited, in the range of 0.4 million to 0.5 million acre-feet each.

Simply summing these strategies overstates the potential, because some—for instance, surface and groundwater storage—could compete for the same supplies or storage and conveyance facilities. However, the estimates exclude two important options: regional and local surface storage projects (for which no figures are available) and water transfers from voluntary reductions in agricultural water use through crop idling (for which estimation has proven contentious).

Advantages and Drawbacks of Different Supply Options

The optimal mix of supply solutions will differ by locality and region, depending on costs, reliability, institutional barriers, and public acceptability. Although there are no systematic data available on costs, the following discussion indicates the relative attractiveness and drawbacks of the main options. Cost estimates presented are for annual deliveries of "raw" water, exclusive of treatment costs to meet drinking water standards. They include the amortized capital costs plus operations and maintenance.

Urban Water-Use Efficiency

Conservation is a demand-side measure to free up supplies. The upper range of estimates on potential water savings comes from a recent study by the Pacific Institute (Gleick et al., 2003), which examined the scope for behavioral changes and new technology to reduce consumption in the residential, commercial, and industrial sectors. It concluded that roughly 12 percent of urban use could be cut back at a cost of $100 per acre-foot or less and as much as 34 percent at less than $600 per acre-foot—a threshold the authors deem relevant for most alternative sources.[11] A substantial volume of new water—over 600,000 acre-feet from current indoor residential use and some portion from outdoor uses—would more than pay for itself thanks to the associated savings in energy (less hot water for low-flow showers and washing machines, and less frequent use of irrigation systems) and other inputs (fewer losses of fertilizer, pesticide, and seeds from overwatering). Significantly, much of the outdoor savings comes from the use of improved technology and husbandry techniques rather than from a reduction in turf. Although the authors advocate urban conservation as the least-cost, most environmentally sound option for providing new water, they acknowledge that there may be considerable "educational, political and social barriers" to achieving these savings. Community resistance to metering and the slow progress toward increasing block rate pricing since the mid-1990s are cases in point.

Recycled Municipal Water

To some, recycling wastewater is just another form of conservation, because it enables a supply augmentation from the initial source.

---

[11]The California Urban Water Agencies (2001, 2004) estimate that implementation of quantifiable BMPs (a narrower set of goals) would generate just over 1 million acre-feet cost-effectively by 2030.

However, quite different issues are at stake. Because most recycled water is not sufficiently processed to meet drinking water standards, it requires separate plumbing. Incremental processing and distribution costs can also be high. Generally limited to outdoor uses, recycled water also risks being in excess supply in wet winter months. As a result of these factors, recycled water is not necessarily a financial bargain. The potential for cost effectiveness is greater for new construction and new treatment plants. The California Recycled Water Task Force (Department of Water Resources, 2003a) estimated average unit costs of expansion on the order of $600 per acre-foot for treatment and delivery.

Battles must also be won to convince the public of the safety of recycled water. There have been several well-publicized cases of public resistance to recycled water use, not only as an indirect source of potable water (through groundwater recharge) but also for some outdoor uses (e.g., in parks and yards where children play). These factors help account for the fact that by the early 2000s, recycled water accounted for only half a million acre-feet per year. The task force's projections of a three- to fourfold expansion over the next few decades assume that utilities will be able to overcome this resistance through public education and outreach. One promising enterprise is Orange County's "Groundwater Replenishment System," which should begin recharging the groundwater basin with 70,000 acre-feet per year of highly purified recycled water in 2007.

Surface Storage

Much of the impetus for expanding the portfolio of water options derives from concerns about the environmental consequences of large surface storage projects. Nevertheless, many hold the view that some expansion of surface storage is necessary in California, particularly in light of predictions that, sooner or later, climate change will reduce the storage capability of the Sierra snow pack.[12] The deliberations on statewide surface storage have taken place under the auspices of CALFED, a joint state-federal program to restore the ecosystem of the

---

[12]For recent analyses of the potential water supply effects of climate change in California, see Lund et al. (2003) and Hayhoe et al. (2004).

San Francisco–San Joaquin Bay Delta while securing water supplies to urban and agricultural users. CALFED's 2000 Record of Decision included an agreement to explore options for five new surface storage projects. For farmers, a key objective is to restore some of the supplies they lost through environmental mitigation in the early 1990s under the CVPIA and other regulatory decisions.

The expansion program remains highly contentious, with most environmental groups opposing expansion, despite claims that the environment could be a primary beneficiary of new storage. Funding has also been a stumbling block. With hoped-for federal contributions lagging, water users have been forced to reexamine the issue of who should pay. Although firm cost numbers are not available, one CALFED study (1999) estimated a range of $150 to $1,000 per acre-foot. It concluded that although some urban agencies would be willing to pay for such water, farmers would require substantial subsidies to use it. Because urban agencies have a range of other cost-effective options, significant taxpayer support would be required to fund expansion at the proposed scale. One central discussion now under way concerns the appropriate level of public subsidies for new storage, given the potential for broader public benefits, including improved capacity to manage environmental flows (CALFED, 2004).

Although less in the spotlight, local and regional projects to expand surface storage and conveyance are a key component of urban supply strategies in some areas. Most notably, the Metropolitan Water District's recently completed Diamond Valley Lake in Riverside County provides a regional storage capacity of 0.8 million acre-feet. Other examples include the pending expansion of water use from Lake Nacimiento in San Luis Obispo County and the upgrade of San Francisco's Hetch-Hetchy system. In contrast to the CALFED projects, which are not viable without general taxpayer funds, these projects are principally funded by local users.

Groundwater Storage and Conjunctive Use

The other storage option is underground, and it involves the conjunctive use of surface and groundwater. Conjunctive use exploits the interannual variability of rainfall by promoting greater use of groundwater in dry years to maximize storage of excess surface water in high rainfall years. Groundwater banking projects can deliver water at very low cost: A representative group of projects recently submitted to DWR for financial support had a weighted average annual cost of $110 per acre-foot, with a range from $10 to $600. Not all of these estimates included the costs of acquiring the surface water for storage, which can vary from negligible to several hundred dollars per acre-foot, depending on the source and the year. The Water Plan estimates that groundwater storage has the potential to generate 0.5 million to 2.0 million acre-feet of new water; reaching the upper end of this range would require changes in the management of surface reservoirs and conveyance systems and possibly also complementary investments in conveyance.

Relative to surface storage, groundwater banking is generally considered an environmentally friendly option. However, it has some potential drawbacks. For one, both storage and retrieval are slower than with surface storage. When the objective is to capture and store a large volume of flood flow during a relatively short amount of time, recharge capacity may be a limiting factor. Similarly, retrieval from groundwater banks is often limited by pumping capacity. Second, water-quality concerns may arise from mixing water from different sources. This presents an obstacle, for instance, to the storage of recycled water in the Mojave Basin and to the storage of treated surface water by the city of Tracy. Contamination from overlying land use (fertilizers and industrial chemicals) also raises water-quality issues for conjunctive use in some areas.

Third, and perhaps most important, groundwater banking can be successful only when there is a sound local management system for the aquifer (Thomas, 2001; Hanak, 2003). Unmanaged basins present risks both to bankers and their neighbors. Bankers run the risk of not being able to retrieve the water they store, and their neighbors run the risk of seeing the aquifer depleted from excessive retrieval. For this reason, most groundwater banking takes place within areas owned or managed by a single entity that can enforce accountability, such as a water master or a special groundwater management district. To date, such basins are mainly located within Southern California and some coastal regions farther north. Major expansion of groundwater banking in Kern County since the mid-1990s has also been facilitated by management protocols. Improvement of groundwater management is a priority elsewhere in the Central Valley, where there is considerable potential for groundwater banking and conjunctive use.

Water Transfers

Water transfers have also been promoted as an option with the potential to be both low-cost and environmentally friendly, and both state and federal policies have actively promoted their use since the early 1990s. Determining the amount available from transfers has been a contentious issue for the Water Plan Update, however, because some agricultural interests argue that transfers do not augment supplies. Some of the strategies listed in Figure 2.5 (agricultural water-use efficiency and groundwater storage) do imply transfer activity. But agricultural water use is also likely to decline because of various market forces, including residential growth and a net shift to higher-value, less-water-using crops. Accordingly, the California Water Plan Update assumes that agricultural demand will be 1.9 million to 3.5 million acre-feet lower in 2030, a 5 to 10 percent drop over demand in 2000 (Groves, Matyac, and Hawkins, 2005). This opens up potential both for transfers and for basin recharge.

Although transfers can raise concerns about negative effects in the source regions, there are already signs of substantial movement in this direction. Of the approximately 1.2 million acre-feet transferred annually by the early 2000s, urban agencies were purchasing only 200,000 to 300,000 acre-feet.[13] A number of recent and pending contracts for long-term and permanent transfers could increase this total by at least 700,000 acre-feet over the coming decade alone.

Legally, transfers must mitigate potential harm to the environment from a change in water flows. To forge deals, buyers and sellers also need to consider the local context, to limit the risk of economic harm to the community from a reduction in agricultural activity. Such concerns have led to the establishment of mitigation funds for some long-term transfers and to rules limiting the amount of fallowing in any given area.

---

[13]For data on historic and pending water market transactions, see Appendix A in Hanak (2003).

Although the lead-time to meet environmental and community requirements can be substantial, transfers do indeed provide a relatively low-cost water source to urban agencies, with prices for delivered water (including the costs of moving it to the buyer's destination) ranging from under $100 per acre-foot for local deals within the Central Valley to $400 per acre-foot for deliveries to cities on the Southern Coast.

Desalination

An option that has gained much media attention in recent years—desalination of ocean water—is now on the drawing board of utilities in a number of coastal communities. Although projected costs have fallen, they remain substantial in comparison with most other options—in the range of $800 to $1,500 per acre-foot according to the Task Force on Water Desalination (Department of Water Resources, 2003b). In Central Coast communities, such as Monterey and Morro Bay, faced with few alternatives, this may still be a good price. By contrast, expansion in San Diego is relying on subsidies from the Metropolitan Water District of $250 per acre-foot.

Desalination of brackish groundwater is already widely practiced in Southern California, producing 170,000 acre-feet of clean water annually, and the task force anticipates that this amount could triple over the coming decades. The costs range from as little as $130 to as much as $1,250 per acre-foot, depending on location. Both types of desalination must find environmentally acceptable ways to dispose of brine or concentrate; ocean water desalination must also mitigate risks to marine organisms at intake valves.

Planning for an Uncertain Future

The general trends and scenarios presented here highlight the inevitable tension between water supply availability and population growth in California over the coming decades. They also provide some sense of the uncertainties involved in planning for the water supply needs of growth. As the scenarios in Figure 2.4 show, the potential range of demand growth is wide, even under the assumption that we can accurately predict population growth rates several decades out. If growth turns out to be higher, or if its distribution across regions is different from current projections, this could put additional pressures on some water agencies and heighten competition for new supply sources.

As Figure 2.5 underscores, there are also uncertainties about the composition of the future water portfolio, given the wide ranges between the high- and low-end projections for some sources. In large part, this reflects unknowns regarding the extent of institutional and financial constraints associated with expanding different options. Additional factors that could diminish the availability of existing supplies include the potential for climate change to reduce the storage role of the Sierra snowpack and the possibility that a major seismic event will flood the Delta, thereby interrupting water transmission to points south. By its nature, a portfolio approach to water supply planning implies some flexibility to adapt by shifting emphasis as obstacles are encountered. Contingency planning for shocks to the system is clearly also key, and it implies a central coordinating role for the state.

Summing Up

If per capita urban water use were to remain at 2000 levels, anticipated population growth would require a 40 percent expansion of urban supplies by 2030. Because interstate obligations and environmental concerns are requiring that some urban agencies cut back on existing sources, the new supply requirements are potentially even larger.

In this context, the trajectory of per capita use becomes a key question. Although plumbing and appliance codes will moderate indoor use in new homes, growth patterns are putting upward pressure on outdoor use, a major share of the total. Half of all new residents are expected to live in the state's three rapidly growing inland valleys, where the harsher climate leads to higher landscaping needs. This pressure is reinforced by the upward trend in construction of single-family homes, which have larger lots.

Among the diverse portfolio of available options, conservation appears to yield some of the largest, most cost-effective "new" supplies—achieved by reducing demand. Utility rate policies can still make major inroads to encourage conservation. At present, only half of the state's residents are served by utilities using increasing block rate pricing. Large portions of the fast-growing Central Valley are not yet metered, and water rates are still quite low in most communities.

A host of other options—including groundwater and surface water storage, water transfers, recycling, and desalination—come with advantages and drawbacks from financial, environmental, and institutional perspectives. The optimal mix for each community will depend on local and regional cost conditions. These planning decisions are the province of local utilities, to whose activities we now turn.

3. Municipal Water Planning: How Are Utilities Faring?

Among western states, California has one of the most longstanding and comprehensive requirements for water planning by local utilities. The Urban Water Management Planning Act ("the Act"), introduced in 1983 and updated numerous times, requires that all large municipal utilities—those serving at least 3,000 connections or supplying at least 3,000 acre-feet of water annually—prepare a wide-ranging planning document every five years. Although many utilities engage in other planning exercises, including water master plans, groundwater management plans, and integrated resource management plans, UWMPs are unique in requiring updates at regular intervals and in providing a standardized checklist of issues to be addressed.

In this chapter, we take advantage of this common framework to provide an overall assessment of utilities' performance in long-term water planning. The analysis draws on a unique database on utilities that were expected to file plans in the most recent UWMP cycle, due at the end of 2000. After describing the major requirements of the Act, we focus on the compliance record and the quality of plans submitted. Although long-time observers note that the planning process has improved considerably since the mid-1980s, performance is not uniformly good. One-sixth of all retailers failed to submit a plan, and there are widespread weaknesses in such key areas as long-term supply and demand planning.

Key Components of Urban Water Management Plans

In light of the many revisions since its inception, the Act itself has become a somewhat unwieldy document, with planning requirements interspersed throughout several dozen sections. To assist utilities in plan preparation, DWR has developed model plans and worksheets. More than a year before the submission deadlines, staff from the Office of Water Use Efficiency and Transfers begin holding workshops and providing technical assistance on the use of the worksheets. The worksheets, model plans, and a variety of other information on UWMPs are available on DWR's website.[1]

For the 2000 plans, the worksheets included nearly 60 required elements: three relating to the process of plan preparation (notably, consultation with the public and other agencies); 17 to a set of topics we have grouped under the heading "supply and demand planning" (demographic factors, detailed and aggregate water supply and use, and supply reliability conditions); 12 to wastewater disposal and recycling opportunities; 11 to the utility's water shortage contingency plan; and 14 to its conservation programs, corresponding to the 14 BMPs promoted by the CUWCC (Appendix Table B.1). Plans submitted since January 2002 must also include a discussion of water-quality issues and additional information on groundwater sources and new water supply projects. Starting in 2005, plans must provide greater detail on the potential use of desalination.

Although many of the elements call for qualitative discussion, a central objective of the plans is to provide a forum for examining current and projected supplies and demands over a 20-year planning horizon, with data broken into five-year intervals. Ten of the 17 supply and demand planning elements require data of this type, as do three of the wastewater and recycling elements. Under the provisions of SB 610 and SB 221, the "show me the water" laws that took effect in 2002, a UWMP providing comprehensive information of this sort can serve as a basis for demonstrating adequate long-term supplies.

Evaluating Compliance

From the outset, utilities have been required to submit their plans to DWR, which engages in a considerable outreach effort to encourage plan submission. However, its oversight responsibility has been quite limited. In 1991, at the height of the last prolonged drought, the Act was amended to require that utilities include a water shortage contingency

---

[1]http://www.owue.water.ca.gov/urbanplan/index.cfm.

plan, and drought assistance became contingent on compliance with this provision. Since 2002, this financial carrot has been extended to receipt of state funds administered by DWR for a range of water-related activities. DWR is responsible for screening the plans, and only utilities whose plans are deemed "complete" are considered eligible for financial assistance.[2] In screening for completeness, the department has limited itself to assessing whether the plans cover the required items, because it does not have authority to evaluate the quality of the information presented.

The department does collect information that can be used to make more detailed assessments of compliance, however. For each UWMP received, staff use the worksheets to enter data not only on whether an element was addressed but also on some of the details in each section, including any volumes reported. For this study, we have merged this database on UWMP content with other information on all utilities expected to submit UWMPs, including characteristics of the utility itself: organizational status (municipal department, special district, or private company), membership in a wholesale supply network and in a managed groundwater basin, and whether the utility is "full service," providing wastewater services as well as water supply. Our database also includes detailed demographic characteristics of retail utility service areas from the 2000 Census.

This rich set of information allows evaluation of the municipal water planning process from a number of perspectives: How well does the law cover the state's populated areas, including those growing the fastest? How do utilities in different regions fare in meeting the law's requirements? Do utility traits, such as size or membership in a wholesale network, affect the likelihood of complying with the law? What about community traits, such as wealth, home ownership, or political participation? How many plans are providing the basic information needed to demonstrate adequate supplies for new development? Where do utilities expect to find new water by 2020, and

---

[2]This provision will expire in January 2006 unless explicitly extended by the legislature.

how does this compare with the sources DWR has identified in the latest California Water Plan Update?

If All Utilities Complied, UWMP Coverage Would Be Good

The first message that emerges from this analysis is that the Act's coverage is quite broad, even though it does not extend to the hundreds of small utilities falling below the 3,000 acre-foot or 3,000 service-connection thresholds. By our calculations, 418 utilities were large enough to meet these size thresholds, including 26 agencies providing only wholesale services (supplying other utilities), 373 retail agencies (supplying households and establishments), and 19 agencies with mixed wholesale and retail functions.

In 2000, UWMP-eligible agencies served at least 86 percent of the state's population (Table 3.1).[3] Coverage was slightly lower for new housing, reflecting faster growth in less developed areas, where utilities

Table 3.1

Geographical Coverage of UWMPs for the 2000 Reporting Cycle

	No. of Retail and Mixed Agencies		% of Population Covered, 2000		% of New Housing Covered, 1990–2000	
	Eligible	Submitted	Eligible	Submitted	Eligible	Submitted
Bay Area	60	46	90	81	82	74
Southern Coast	149	138	93	89	92	90
Central Coast	28	21	66	51	57	41
Inland Empire	51	43	87	80	82	74
San Joaquin Valley	43	27	65	33	61	36
Sacramento Metro	26	24	80	80	76	75
Rest of the state	34	20	53	34	56	38
California	391	319	86	77	79	70

NOTES: The table excludes one retailer in the Southern Coast region for which service area data were not available. Submission count is as of July 2003.

---

[3]Our estimate is conservative because some of the service area maps date back to the mid-1990s; if any subsequent annexations occurred, this would increase coverage. Also, some areas may be covered by a wholesale plan even though they are not served by a retail agency large enough to fall under the provisions of the UWMP Act.

may not yet meet the size threshold. However, as of July 2003—two and a half years after the deadline for plan submission—72 of these utilities (18%) had yet to submit a UWMP. Accordingly, actual UWMP reporting was somewhat lower, with only 77 percent of the population and 70 percent of new housing covered by plans. These rates rose slightly over the following year.[4] Although performance has improved since 1995, when only 75 percent of all agencies submitted plans, there is still a clear margin for progress (Department of Water Resources, 1998).

Coverage rates vary considerably by region. Eligible utilities serve a large share of population and new housing in the state's two coastal metropolitan regions as well as in the Inland Empire and the Sacramento Metro region. Coverage is lower in regions with smaller towns and traditionally more rural development patterns—the Central Coast, the San Joaquin Valley, and counties in the rest of the state. Actual submission rates are particularly low in these last two regions. As a result, in the fast-growing San Joaquin Valley, less than two-fifths of population and new housing are covered by a plan.

Rates of Compliance for Wholesale Agencies Are Generally High

Agencies providing wholesale deliveries of at least 3,000 acre-feet annually have been required to submit plans since the early 1990s, even if they have no retail customers. All 26 wholesalers considered eligible under the law submitted plans. Two of the 19 mixed agencies failed to do so. The level of plan completeness varies for wholesale suppliers, much as it does for retail agencies (Appendix Table B.1).

It is also worth noting that the law does not require plans from some agencies that provide important water management oversight functions, as long as they do not technically purvey water. This group includes several county agencies that administer State Water Project supplies for

---

[4]Between July 2003 and August 2004, another nine eligible utilities, in six of the seven regions, submitted plans. This raised coverage to 84 percent of eligible retailers, 78 percent of the population, and 72 percent of new housing. Because we do not have detailed reporting data on these late submitters, the analysis here concentrates on the plans submitted by July 2003.

local retail agencies (e.g., Santa Barbara, Ventura, Napa) and nearly 20 agencies managing the use of adjudicated or special district groundwater basins in southern and coastal regions. Among groundwater management agencies, only one—the Santa Clara Valley Water District (SCVWD)—submitted a UWMP, because it also provides broader wholesale services.

Membership in a wholesale network is common in California: Statewide, only one-third of the UWMP-eligible retail agencies are independent. However, the rates vary widely by region, with the vast majority of Bay Area and Southern Coast utilities in networks, versus half or fewer in other regions (Appendix Table B.4). The San Joaquin Valley again stands out, with only one-fifth of eligible retailers in a wholesale network. The largest wholesale network in the state by far (and, indeed, the country) is headed by MWDSC. Through its 26 wholesale and retail member agencies, it spans 142 of the 200 eligible retail providers in the Southern Coast and Inland Empire regions, covering nearly 15.5 million residents in 2000. The two large San Francisco Bay Area networks, headed by the San Francisco Public Utilities Commission (SFPUC) and the SCVWD, are dwarfed by comparison, with 25 and 10 network members, respectively, and a combined population in 2000 of 3.3 million residents. Wholesale agencies typically furnish only a portion of a retailer's water supply, with the rest mobilized through local surface water rights, groundwater withdrawals, and such other projects as recycling. For instance, during the 1990s, MWDSC provided roughly half of total supplies for its large service area, and it expects the local share to increase over the coming decades.[5]

Membership in adjudicated or special district groundwater basin networks is less common, covering about one-third of utilities statewide, and heavily skewed toward the two southern regions and the coastal areas farther north.[6] In adjudicated basins, members are allocated specific annual quantities; in special groundwater management districts, the district regulates supply by charging pump fees.

---

[5]Metropolitan Water District of Southern California (2000).

[6]For a map showing adjudicated basins and special groundwater management districts, see Hanak (2003).

Determinants of Retail Utility Compliance

A number of utility and community traits might be expected to influence the planning performance of utilities providing retail services. Here, we discuss some of the hypotheses regarding these factors and describe the indicators available to measure them. We then present the results of the analysis of performance for our sample of 391 UWMP-eligible retail agencies. The analysis employs multiple regression techniques, which isolate the effect of each factor on utility performance, controlling for the effects of all other factors.[7]

It seems reasonable to expect that wholesale supply networks should exert a positive influence on the planning activities of member agencies. These networks should enable members to reap some economies of scale in planning as well as in the organization of supply sources. We might expect member benefits to be greatest when the wholesaler itself plays a leadership role, an effect we will measure by the completeness of the wholesaler's UWMP.

Other utility characteristics are also likely to affect planning quality. Size could play a positive role, if it enables the utility to spread out the fixed costs of planning operations. Full-service utilities might be expected to conduct more sophisticated water resource planning, given their need to jointly consider water and wastewater supply, treatment, and disposal. Forty percent of the retail and mixed utilities in our sample also provide wastewater services, at least for a portion of their service area.

There has also been some speculation regarding the extent to which organizational form affects performance. At issue are questions of efficiency, transparency, and public responsiveness of special districts, private utilities, and municipal water departments. As noted above, the California landscape is quite diverse in this respect. Among eligible utilities providing retail services, 50 percent are municipal departments, 32 percent are special districts, and 18 percent are privately owned.[8]

---

[7] For a discussion of data and methods, see Appendix B.

[8] Most pure wholesalers are special districts, although several are county-run agencies.

The potential tradeoffs between a special district and a local general-purpose government management structure have received attention both from political scientists and from California watchdog entities such as the Little Hoover Commission (2000).[9] Special districts, with their specialized boards, dedicated budgets, and limited scope of activities, may have an upper hand from the efficiency standpoint. By comparison, city water departments must compete with other departments for funding and for the attention of city council members. However, some analysts have argued that special districts may be less transparent and responsive, because they operate out of the limelight of public scrutiny.[10] Similar arguments have been made both for and against private utilities: They should share special districts' advantages on the efficiency criterion (or, indeed, outperform them); yet they raise concerns from the standpoint of transparency.[11]

In addition to these utility traits, we might expect characteristics of the community to influence the quality of water planning. In particular, if members of the community have a higher stake in the outcome, they may put more pressure on utilities to comply with planning laws. More generally, a more politically active community might exact higher standards of performance from local officials. These community traits are less straightforward to measure than are the utility traits noted above. We measure the community's stake in the outcome with two indicators of home equity: the median home price and the share of homeowners. Home prices are also a broader indicator of community wealth. A third,

---

[9]See, for instance, Ostrom, Bish, and Ostrom (1988), Foster (1997), and Mullin (2003).

[10]The argument here is that the multiplicity of special districts and the frequent practice of holding district elections outside regular electoral cycles reduce transparency. Others have argued that special districts may be more responsive than general-purpose governments, because their elections allow a vote on district performance with respect to a narrow set of community issues, whereas general local elections require that voters pick leaders based on different views on a wide array of issues. Mullin (2003) provides a discussion of the literature.

[11]The National Research Council (2002) provides evidence that private service providers are more efficient than public agencies by some criteria. Citizen groups concerned with transparency and accountability have led the battles against privatization of some California utilities, such as the Stockton Water Department.

more direct, measure of political participation is the share of eligible adults registered to vote in the November 2000 elections.[12]

We are also interested in seeing whether communities facing greater growth pressures are more or less likely to comply with state laws on water planning. On the one hand, growth pressure might induce better planning, particularly if it mobilizes community interest; on the other hand, rapid growth may catch the utility and the community unawares, especially if it is occurring in outlying areas with limited institutional capacity. Finally, a regional measure is included to capture any systematic differences across regions not reflected in the variables noted here. This would capture, for instance, the regional differences in reliance on imported water. Higher import dependency might lead utilities to place more emphasis on long-term planning.

Our analysis focuses on several summary measures of overall performance: whether the utility submitted a plan; an "overall compliance" score that tallies how many of the nearly 60 required elements the utility's plan contains; and a "volume data" score measuring the availability of 13 key data series in the plan.[13] Clearly, completeness does not guarantee that plans are good; this also depends on the quality of the analysis for each subject area. But availability of information is a prerequisite to a good planning document.

Utility Characteristics Are Key for Planning Performance

As a group, the variables capturing utility characteristics are the most significant determinants of plan performance. Wholesale network membership and operation as a full-service utility exert the expected, positive effect. Utilities whose wholesaler has a complete UWMP are 16 percent more likely than those with no wholesaler plan to have submitted their own UWMP; their overall compliance scores are 29 percent higher, and their plans contain 19 percent more volume data (or

---

[12]This measure of political participation proved more robust than several alternatives (see Appendix B).

[13]See Appendix Table B.2 for details on the results discussed here.

more than two additional data series).[14] Although full-service operation does not affect submission rates, it has significant effects on both measures of plan quality. By contrast, utility size, measured by the number of households served, does not appear to matter. This suggests that California's utilities mainly benefit from scale economies in planning through their wholesale networks, not their own size.

Organizational form also emerges as a significant factor. In comparison with special districts, municipal departments and private utilities register lower submission and completion rates. Private utilities are at the bottom of the pyramid: They are nearly 20 percent less likely than special districts to submit a plan, and their plans provide nearly 40 percent less volume data. City departments do somewhat better on providing planning data but are still outperformed by special districts. These findings lend some weight to the view that special districts, with their dedicated focus on water-related activities, are in a better position than general-purpose local governments to meet professional standards. Because plans are public documents, these results also counter the view that special districts are less transparent than municipal governments in this area.

The relatively poor performance of private utilities could lend weight to critics of the investor-owned form of utility management. However, it is important to note that private utilities have not had the same set of incentives to comply with the law as either special districts or municipal departments. The financial carrot introduced by SB 610 applies only to public water utilities, because private utilities have not been eligible for state bond funding. Although this does not excuse private utilities from complying with the Act, it does suggest that financial incentives may play a positive role in encouraging compliance. The Legislative Analyst's Office (2004) has recently argued that private utilities should become eligible for bond funding on equity grounds, since their customers, like other Californians, must contribute to bond repayment. The potential

---

[14]Although membership in a wholesale network also exerts a positive influence, the *quality* of the wholesaler's plan (measured by the availability of volume data) has greater explanatory power.

incentive for encouraging long-term planning may be another justification for relaxing this restriction.

For Communities, Political Participation Is Key

Broad-based political participation improves the planning process. In communities with higher-than-average rates of voter registration, utilities are more likely to submit plans, and their plans are more complete. However, communities with higher home values and home ownership rates do not appear more successful in pressuring their utilities to comply with water planning laws. Wealthier communities are in fact slightly *less* likely to comply. The key to this somewhat surprising result is the role of other factors. In a simple comparison of compliance rates by wealth quintiles, utilities with the poorest households are also the worst performers. However, low-wealth service areas also tend to have lower rates of membership in wholesale networks and lower rates of voter registration. These two factors turn out to be more important than wealth in explaining utility performance.

The UWMP consultation process provides further evidence of the importance of public participation. Recall that one plan requirement is to describe the coordination of plan preparation with other agencies and the public. Planning quality—using our two measures of plan completeness—is significantly influenced by this outreach activity. Plans are better not only when utilities involve other agencies (other water and wastewater utilities and local governments), but also when they involve representatives of the public (citizen groups, public and special interest groups, and the general public) (Appendix Table B.6). Not surprisingly, utilities whose communities have higher rates of general political participation—as measured by voter registration—have significantly higher rates of public outreach (Appendix Table B.7). But outreach is also higher in communities with lower rates of home ownership and lower home values. Special districts engage in more pubic outreach than either municipal departments or private utilities, again challenging the view that they are less transparent.

These findings are encouraging, because they suggest that low-wealth communities are not necessarily at a disadvantage when it comes to long-term water planning. Going forward, efforts to encourage public awareness and participation in the planning process should continue to play a positive role.

Growth Pressures and Regional Patterns

Finally, our analysis shows that utilities experiencing the greatest growth pressures are neither more nor less likely to engage in long-term planning. None of our measures of growth pressure are significantly associated with either plan submission or plan completeness. However, one region does stand out, even after controlling for the full range of utility and community characteristics. Utilities in Southern California (the four coastal counties and the two counties of the Inland Empire) have higher compliance rates for submission and plan completion.[15] In light of this region's considerable growth pressures, its high dependency on water imported from other regions, and its pending loss of surplus Colorado River water, the better planning scores come as good news. They suggest that, on the whole, the region's utilities are taking these challenges seriously.

By contrast, the San Joaquin Valley does not register a significant regional effect, even though submission rates there are lower than in all other regions except the rural counties in the rest of the state. Poor performance in this fast-growing region can instead be attributed to utility and community characteristics: lower rates of membership in wholesale networks, a greater predominance of municipal utilities, and lower rates of political participation.

Supply and Demand Planning

We now turn the spotlight on a central planning objective of the UWMPs—projections of long-term supply and demand. One question is whether agencies are providing the data needed to gauge whether their community's water needs can be met. Another is how reliable these data are. There has been considerable concern in some circles, for instance, that utilities are planning with "paper water"—as-yet-unused water for

---

[15]The regional effect for Southern California is *not* attributable to membership in the MWDSC network. When MWDSC membership is included in the regressions, it is insignificant, and the regional variable retains its size and significance.

which they theoretically may have use rights but which will be difficult to access in practice because of competition from other users.

Data Availability and Quality Issues

Availability rates for key series suggest that California's utilities still have a way to go (Figure 3.1). Among utilities providing retail services, 84 percent are able to project detailed sources of supply out to 2020. This number falls to 63 percent for projections of demand by customer category (residential, commercial, etc.). Taken together, only 58 percent of submitted plans provide this information for both supply and demand.

Drawing a complete picture of the quality of this planning data would require in-depth assessment of each plan, a task beyond the scope of this study. However, it is possible to provide some insights on data reliability. Overall, the results suggest further limitations to the usefulness of the UWMPs for long-term planning.

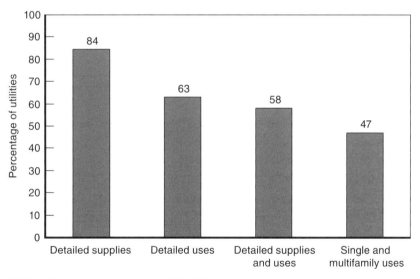

NOTE: The figure reports data for 319 utilities providing retail services that submitted UWMPs as of July 2003.

Figure 3.1—Availability of Supply and Demand Projections to 2020

One indicator of planning quality is the method used to project demand. Given the importance of outdoor water use in total residential demand, water planning experts prefer demand projections based on land-use patterns rather than on population alone (Johnson and Loux, 2004). Ideally, the utility would use projections from a document such as the general plan, taking into account zoning for lot sizes as well as large landscaping needs (parks and golf courses).[16] At a minimum, considering the different needs of single and multifamily residences can provide much more accurate residential use projections than population data can. Judging by the data reported, fewer than half of all retailers make this distinction (Figure 3.1).

Another quality indicator is the consistency of data reporting. In addition to providing disaggregated projections for both supply and demand, the plans are supposed to compare total levels of supply and demand out to 2020. For a surprisingly large share of utilities, wide discrepancies exist between these two sets of numbers. In all, we find that only a third of the submitted plans have consistent data, with both supply and demand sources differing by less than 10 percent.

Some utilities report actual supply sources in one series and theoretical or paper sources in the other. Alternatively, they report the entire supply for their wholesaler in one case and the supplies they actually have access to in another. Meanwhile, many wholesalers report inconsistent figures on demand and supply in their service area, in one case showing the amount they expect to provide their members and in another the total demand and supply, including other sources. In some cases, the discrepancies arise for no apparent reason. Typically, no explanation is given of why the data series differ.

Switching back and forth between wholesaler and retailer data is problematic for supply and demand forecasting, because it leaves some ambiguity in the extent to which the wholesaler will be able to cover demands in a specific retail service area. This is a particular issue with respect to the new state laws requiring the demonstration of long-term

---

[16]For example, the East Bay Municipal Utilities District revises its projections using general and specific plan updates within its service area. Improvements in geographic information systems software should make it easier for utilities to move toward such methods.

water availability to approve new development. UWMPs may not stand up to challenges if they do not convincingly address water availability in the retail service area, including the amounts likely to be supplied by the wholesaler. Similar issues arise when the utility is counting on the availability of paper water to meet future demands, a problem to which we return below.

Adding Up the Numbers

What overall picture emerges from the utilities' supply and demand analysis? First, the numbers on current demand—implying a use rate of 240 gallons per capita per day in 2000—are quite close to DWR's statewide estimates for the Water Plan Update (Table 3.2).[17] On the whole, this suggests that the UWMPs are providing a fairly accurate

Table 3.2

Per Capita Water Use, 2000 and 2020 (gpcd)

	2000	2020
Bay Area	226	234
Central Coast	200	169
Southern Coast	200	200
Inland Empire	339	272
San Joaquin Valley	329	373
Sacramento Metro	360	382
Rest of the state	789	671
California[a]	240	246

NOTES: Calculations are based on demand reporting from a sample of 266 UWMPs. We took the higher series when the plans showed discrepancies between detailed and total demand. See Appendix B.

[a]The statewide figure is a population-weighted average, treating the rest-of-the-state region as though it has average use levels.

---

[17]DWR's estimates, presented in Table 2.4, are derived from a separate utility survey, calibrated with a statewide flow balance model.

snapshot of current urban water use. Second, most utilities are not projecting substantial conservation savings between now and 2020. Per capita use would decline only in the Central Coast and the Inland Empire and would actually increase in several other regions, bringing total use up by several gallons per capita per day.

Instead, utilities are banking on increases in new supplies of nearly 3.4 million acre-feet from a diverse set of sources (Figure 3.2).[18] The largest single source is groundwater pumping, accounting for a third of the total. Another is recycled water, which would more than triple in volume. By contrast, retail agencies do not anticipate major increases in surface water from state, federal, and local projects. They do expect large gains from their wholesalers, however. Some wholesalers, such as MWDSC, anticipate substantial surface water increases of their own

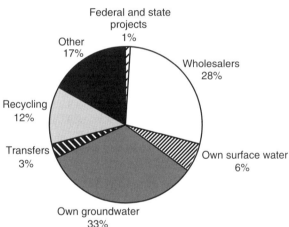

Total increase: 3.35 million acre-feet

NOTES: Statewide estimates are based on an extrapolation from 242 utilities with retail service in all regions except the rest-of-the-state region. For details, see Appendix Table B.8.

Figure 3.2—Retail Utilities' Anticipated Supply Increases, 2000–2020

[18]This figure would be lower if the UWMPs had been developed after DOF's downward revision in population forecasts. As shown in Figure 2.4, constant per capita water use is now projected to require an increase in supplies of 3.6 million acre-feet by 2030.

from the State Water Project, an outcome that would require increased pumping through the Delta. Southern California wholesalers are also counting on large surface water transfers to augment supplies.

Projected increases in recycling may be taken as a sign that utilities are moving away from a "business as usual" mode of water planning toward more integrated approaches. At the same time, the significant planned increase in groundwater pumping could raise concerns, given continuing problems of overdraft in many basins. By our estimates, just over a third of this increase is slated to occur within fully managed basins, where the management entity undertakes to ensure adequate recharge. Close to half of the increase is projected for utilities in the San Joaquin Valley and Sacramento Metro region, where a more loosely run groundwater management movement has been gaining ground, with the formation of multiagency groundwater management plans and joint powers authorities.[19] Although some of these groups are moving toward quantifying rights or establishing pump fees, most still rely on voluntary agreements. To avoid continued overdraft as these regions accommodate growth, these groups will need to play an increasingly effective role.

Margin of Comfort or Paper Water?

A final point of concern with the utility supply data relates to the total volumes reported. A substantial share of retailers show excess supplies both now and into the future (Figure 3.3). In 2000, 62 percent of the sample indicated supplies at least 10 percent higher than demand, and this share barely drops for 2020. In 2020, a full fifth of utilities expect to enjoy a surplus of at least 50 percent. A particularly high share of utilities in the Sacramento Metro region and the rest of the state report large surpluses.

By contrast, the share of utilities showing supply deficits is relatively low: 8 percent in 2000, moving to 9 percent in 2020. Although some of these deficits may result from rounding errors or the use of inconsistent data sources, in other cases they reflect utility concerns

---

[19]Department of Water Resources (2003d) and Hanak (2003) discuss these trends in groundwater management.

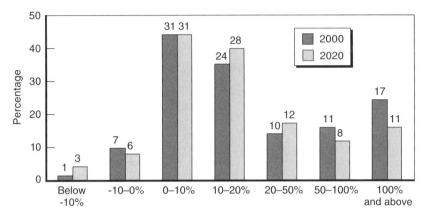

NOTE: Excess supply is calculated as the percentage by which supply exceeds demand. The intervals close just below the higher number. The sample includes 266 utilities with retail service and at least one supply and demand series. Calculations were made using the higher supply or demand series when more than one series was available. Agencies were excluded from the sample when there was a clear confusion between retailer and wholesaler volumes or other data reporting errors.

Figure 3.3—Utilities' Current and Projected Excess Water Supply, 2000 and 2020

about limited supplies. For instance, the city of Oxnard (Ventura County) projects a deficit of over 40 percent by 2020 with currently identifiable sources.

The large share of utilities with surpluses could be taken as a positive sign, implying a considerable margin of comfort to meet demands under drought conditions or an unforeseen rise in water demand. However, it should also raise a red flag because, in the aggregate, it implies that urban utilities are laying claim to a much greater amount of water than they are actually using. In both 2000 and 2020, the excess supply figures for the utilities in this sample, which served just under two-thirds of the 2000 population, come in at roughly 1.7 million acre-feet. Allowing for nonreporting utilities, the collective surplus could easily lie above 2 million acre-feet. California's water system simply does not have this kind of slack: For utilities to access these surpluses, they would need to be supplanting some other agricultural, urban, or environmental users.

Summing Up

Under the terms of the Urban Water Management Planning Act, California's large utilities are required to undertake detailed long-term planning exercises every five years. The evidence from the latest planning cycle suggests some positive signs but also much room for improvement. The Act's potential coverage is broad, reaching nearly 90 percent of the state's population and 80 percent of new housing. The failure of one-sixth of eligible utilities to submit plans reduces this coverage somewhat, however. With smaller utilities and lower compliance rates, the fast-growing San Joaquin Valley is in the tenuous position of having only two-fifths of its population covered by plans. Statewide, essential long-term planning data, including both individual supply sources and the likely composition of demand, are missing in over 40 percent of all plans submitted.

When we add up the numbers that are available, the plans tell a somewhat different story about future demand and supply than the one emerging from the California Water Plan Update. First, utilities are projecting demand and supply increases that would essentially allow per capita consumption to remain unchanged between now and 2020, in effect neglecting the potential for conservation to generate new water. Second, increased groundwater pumping is projected to be the largest component of new supplies—a practice likely to aggravate overdraft in the Central Valley and some unadjudicated Southern California basins unless local efforts to manage groundwater basins are reinforced considerably. Finally, both now and in the future, the majority of utilities are reporting substantial excess supplies. Although some margin of comfort is certainly desirable, the magnitudes involved—some 2 million acre-feet per year—suggest that many utilities are banking on paper water already being used by someone else within the state's water system.

There is some rhyme and reason to the patterns of compliance with water planning law. Both the likelihood of submission and the completeness of planning documents are related to utility and community characteristics. In particular, membership in a wholesale network and the *quality* of the wholesaler's own plan—as measured by the extent of data it provides—greatly improve the performance of retail providers. Full-service utilities, managing both water and wastewater services, are also at an advantage. Communities in which political participation is higher are more likely to perform well, a result confirmed by the higher scores of utilities that engage in public outreach while preparing their plans. These findings lend weight to recent state policy efforts to promote regional water management initiatives and to encourage greater public involvement in the water planning process.

Another factor influencing performance is the utility's organizational form. Utilities constituted as special districts do significantly better than either city water departments or private utilities. Special districts are also the most likely to engage in public outreach. These results provide some counterweight to the view that special districts are less transparent than general-purpose local governments. They suggest instead that as a group, special districts are doing a better job meeting their professional obligations.

Somewhat different questions arise when we consider the ability of local entities to conduct more integrated resource planning, however. As planning scholars have long pointed out, coordination may be more difficult when water supply planning is conducted by an entity separate from the local government responsible for land use. This is one of the issues we address in the next chapter, which shifts the focus from water planning to ensuring water and land-use linkages at the local level.

4. Linking Water and Land Use: How Big Is the Disconnect?

Whereas utilities are responsible for ensuring local water supplies, cities and counties are responsible for the land-use decisions that critically affect local demand. General and specific plans, subdivision approval, and zoning help shape not only the overall size of communities but also the density and landscaping patterns that planners sometimes refer to as their "footprint."

California law imposes a fairly stringent set of planning requirements on the city and county governments responsible for land-use oversight. Comprehensive general plans are supposed to be updated every 10 years, and specific plans must be developed for projects deemed to have potentially significant local impacts. Since 1970, the California Environmental Quality Act (CEQA) has subjected these plans to environmental review, under which projects may be altered, or even blocked, if they cause environmental harm. This review should include an analysis of the project's effects on water supply and groundwater.[1]

By the early 1990s, critics began asserting that this review process was insufficiently rigorous, letting large projects fall through the cracks. The "poster child" was the 11,000-unit Dougherty Valley development in the unincorporated part of Contra Costa County.[2] County officials had approved the project, which lay outside any utility's service area, on the assumption that it would be served by the East Bay Municipal Utilities District. EBMUD, which had not been consulted, took the county to court, arguing that it could not reliably meet demands within

---

[1]Specifically, this requirement is laid out in CEQA's "Initial Study Checklist."

[2]For a discussion of the legal cases associated with this project, see Waterman (2004).

its current service area if it were required to take on this new responsibility. Although EBMUD prevailed in court, the experience prompted the agency to push for legislation to preclude this type of uncoordinated planning in the future. These efforts culminated in the 2001 passage of the "show me the water" laws—SB 610 and SB 221—requiring review of long-term water availability for large projects, with joint involvement of land-use agencies and utilities.

The public debates leading up to and following the passage of these laws have focused on the pros and cons of the legislation itself: Are the review thresholds (above 500 units) too high? Will pro-growth local agencies and builders circumvent the rules by proposing projects that fall below the threshold? Or, alternatively, will antigrowth groups use the legislation as a tool to limit new housing, irrespective of local water supply conditions? Meanwhile, there has been relatively little emphasis on the local policy context. The Dougherty Valley case illustrates a clear disconnect between local land-use authorities and the local utility. Is this type of problem commonplace across the state, or is coordination the rule rather than the exception?

In this chapter, we draw on a recent statewide survey of city and county land-use planners to examine the local linkages between water and land-use planning.[3] We start with some basic questions about agency interaction: Are land-use and water planners talking to each other and sharing information? We then turn to the issue of water supply screening for new development. First, how widespread are local policies in this area, and second, how have the new state laws changed agency behavior? As a backdrop to this discussion, the chapter begins by examining the basis for regulating water and land-use planning linkages.

Why Regulate?

Given the water demand repercussions of land-use decisions, planning and legal scholars and practitioners have long considered the

---

[3]Detailed information about the survey, which took place between November 2003 and February 2004, is provided in Hanak and Simeti (2004). The overall response rate was 59 percent (315 out of 534 jurisdictions), with a representative sample by agency type (city or county), region, and size.

institutional split between utilities and land-use authorities problematic, and many have argued for better linkages.[4] One way to impose linkages is by requiring that land-use authorities explicitly consider water availability in their general planning documents, for instance, through inclusion of a "water element." This step is now required in a handful of states, including Arizona, Washington, and Florida, but it remains optional in California.[5] Such laws as SB 610 and SB 221 are perhaps a less comprehensive means of linking water and land use but are arguably a more direct route. Instead of focusing on the general planning process, they focus on the outcomes for specific projects.

Economic theory is relevant for identifying why such regulations may be justified. In particular, they can be viewed as an attempt to correct a market failure deriving from differences in access to information ("informational asymmetries") and differences in incentive structures between those making building decisions and those who will have to live with the consequences.

The first asymmetry relates to a classic consumer protection issue: the possibility that developers might sell structures lacking basic services to unwitting homebuyers. This scenario is most likely in outlying areas, where new homes depend on individual or community wells.[6] Without disclosure requirements, developers may not have the incentive to inform homebuyers that the water resource base is too limited to provide a reliable supply in the future. Regulation protects these consumers from an investment loss, because home values would fall once the problem became apparent.

These negative impacts will rarely concern only new homebuyers, however. In areas dependent on domestic wells, new building decisions

---

[4]See, for instance, Sanders and Thurow (1982), Ashton and Bayer (1983), Glennon (1991), Sakrison (1995), Lucero (1999), Page (2001), and Speir and Stephenson (2002).

[5]Waterman (2004) and Johnson and Loux (2004) discuss advantages of water elements. The latest general plan guidelines include an optional water element (Governor's Office of Planning and Research, 2003).

[6]Concerns over "dry-lot" development were the motivation for early legislation in Arizona (1972) and Colorado (1973) (Hanak and Browne, 2004). In California, regulation of minimum well standards in outlying areas—including water availability as well as quality—has increased in recent years under the supervision of the Department of Health Service's Office of Drinking Water.

are likely to affect water availability for existing homeowners overlying the same aquifer. In the more common case where new homes are connected to existing utilities, new development may reduce the long-term reliability of water supplies for existing residents. In systems depending on variable surface water, dry-year shortages will become more common. In systems depending on groundwater, the risk of long-term aquifer depletion is heightened.

Herein lies the second asymmetry: Neither builders nor potential new homebuyers have incentives to fully take into account these consequences for existing residents. Without regulation, the incentives are lowest for builders, whose liability ends once the homes are sold. Although new homeowners will also be affected by future shortages, they will share any costs of redressing them with the wider community. For this reason, simple disclosure requirements to new homebuyers may be an inadequate form of regulation.

Local land-use authorities should take the bigger picture into account, because their mission is to be concerned with the long-term economic health of the community at large. But two factors suggest that they may not always do so. First, if the ultimate responsibility for customer service rests with a separate water utility, as in the Dougherty Valley case, land-use authorities may not be led to adequately considering the water supply consequences of growth. Second, even in jurisdictions with municipal water departments, elected officials may take a shorter-term view of resource adequacy than area residents do. If—as is often asserted—land-use authorities are aligned with pro-development forces, they may be inclined to favor growth, even if it means higher costs (or a loss in property values) to the community down the road. Considerations of this type have prompted state legislatures across the West to introduce water supply adequacy requirements to complement or strengthen local screening procedures.

Thus, requirements to demonstrate water availability for new development may correct a market failure, inducing local governments to engage in long-term resource planning and developers to take into account the effects of growth on local water supplies. As with any regulatory process, however, there are also risks of overcorrection. The most obvious risk—raised by opponents of the legislation in California and elsewhere—is that antigrowth advocates may use the requirements as a pretext for limiting growth, irrespective of water supply conditions. A more nuanced version of this problem arises if communities choose to maintain high levels of per household water availability (and low water prices) rather than make room for new residents through conservation. In either case, the regulations then serve as growth controls but not as tools for more efficient management of water resources. We return to these issues in the following chapter, which examines the effects of water adequacy screening policies on housing growth.

Local Government Involvement in Water Planning: A Glass Half Full?

As a first step in gauging the linkages between water utilities and local land-use authorities, our survey asked whether city and county land-use planners were (1) aware of planning documents projecting future water demands, (2) taking part in the planning activities of their water utility(ies), and (3) active in other water policy groups. The survey did not permit a detailed assessment of the quality of these linkages. That said, the overall results suggest that the level of contact is fairly high, although there is certainly room for improvement.

Availability of Water Planning Documents

One basic building block for linking land-use decisions with water planning is information on how projected demographic growth will affect local water demand. This information can be found in utility planning documents as well as in land-use planning documents, such as general plans. The survey aimed to gauge planners' awareness of such documents as well as the type of documents they consult. Overall, seven out of 10 planners reported familiarity with at least one document. For cities with their own utilities, the rate jumped to 86 percent, versus 68 percent for counties and only 53 percent for cities with nonmunicipal water suppliers (Table 4.1). Planners in larger jurisdictions (measured by population) were more likely than those working in smaller communities to identify such documents.

Table 4.1

Planners Reporting Availability of Documents Assessing Future Water Demands

	Cities with Own Water Department	Other Cities	Counties	All
Sample size	159	121	35	315
Share of jurisdictions reporting (%)				
Both water and land-use agency documents	32	5	34	22
Water agency documents only	45	21	17	33
Land-use agency documents only	9	27	17	17
No sources reported	14	47	32	28

SOURCE: PPIC land-use planner survey.

Utility planning documents—including water master plans, UWMPs, and other water resource studies—were the most prevalent sources cited, mentioned 55 percent of the time. Land-use agency documents are nevertheless a significant store of information on water demand, mentioned four times in 10. Among these, the predominant tool is the general plan.[7] This finding is particularly noteworthy in light of recent proposals to require a water element in general plans, because it suggests that many communities have begun to move in this direction.[8] Within the plans, there is a great deal of diversity in the location of water demand analysis. Elements mentioned include land use, public or community facilities/services, conservation, open space, natural resources, environment, housing, circulation, and capital improvements. Only one city (San Luis Obispo) and one county (Los Angeles) specifically mentioned a water and wastewater element.

---

[7]Other sources include Local Agency Formation Commission (LAFCO) municipal service reviews and Environmental Impact Reviews (EIRs) for large-area development projects.

[8]In 2003, AB 1015 proposed to make a water element mandatory. Various interests opposed the move, on grounds that it fell within the five-year cooling-off period on new legislation in this area, an informally negotiated condition of their consent to the passage of SB 221 in 2001.

Cities with their own water departments are nearly 50 percent more likely to mention a utility planning document, but they are no more likely than other jurisdictions to mention a land-use planning document. Because there is no evidence that municipal water departments actually generate more planning tools than other utilities, this pattern suggests that the lines of communication are stronger between land-use and utility planners in cities with their own water departments. (Recall that for UWMPs, city departments actually performed less well than special districts.)

Participation in Utility Planning Activities

A significant majority of city and county land-use departments report that they participate in the planning activities of their water utilities (Table 4.2). Again, having both functions under the same municipal roof appears to matter. Three-quarters of the cities with their own water departments participate, versus only half of the cities with other suppliers. For all agencies, the most common forms of participation are data sharing and review of documents prepared by the utility. Half of the cities with their own water departments take active part in the analysis itself, double the rate of other cities. Other forms of participation include joint management or review of water development projects, joint governance (e.g., sitting on the utility board), and LAFCO service reviews.

Table 4.2

Land-Use Agency Participation in Local Utility Planning Activities

	Cities with Own Water Departments	Other Cities	Counties	All
Number participating	121	58	17	194
Share participating (%)	76	48	49	62
Methods of participation (%)				
Data sharing	79	76	76	79
Review of documents	78	71	88	77
Joint analysis	48	26	35	41
Other	10	10	24	12

SOURCE: PPIC land-use planner survey.

NOTE: Sample size = 315.

Because planners indicated which utilities they were collaborating with, the survey also allows us to explore whether other utility characteristics make a difference to the level of interaction. Seen from this angle, participation rates were slightly lower, because not all utilities serving a jurisdiction engaged the land-use planners. Overall, land-use agencies reported participation in planning for 43 percent of the 458 utilities serving the sample area, with joint analysis occurring 18 percent of the time (Table 4.3). Participation rates were highest in the Bay Area, the Central Coast, and the Inland Empire. City water departments were 25 percent more likely than other utilities to involve land-use planners and 17 percent more likely to engage them in joint analysis. Utilities with better plans, as measured by the completeness of UWMPs, were also more likely to have involved land-use planners in general participation as well as in joint analysis.

In principle, land-use agency involvement in utility planning is most important for the characterization of water demand. The survey results confirm the positive contribution of city and county planners in this

Table 4.3

Utilities Engaging Land-Use Agencies in the Planning Process

	No. of Utilities	Any Participation (%)	Joint Analysis (%)
Bay Area	54	60	35
Central Coast	47	56	29
Southern Coast	122	39	16
Inland Empire	34	59	28
San Joaquin Valley	68	39	17
Sacramento Metro	23	45	15
Rest of the state	111	30	7
California	458	43	18

SOURCE: PPIC land-use planner survey.

NOTES: The sample includes all utilities designated by the land-use planners as providing service within their jurisdiction. It excludes some very small water suppliers serving remote unincorporated areas.

process. Recall from our analysis of UWMP performance in Chapter 3 that only 47 percent of retailers were able to project detailed demands to 2020 reflecting the composition of the housing stock. Utilities that conduct joint analysis with land-use agencies perform significantly better on this score; they are 14 percent more likely to include housing-based projections in their plans. These results highlight, once again, the importance of agency interaction for the quality of long-term water planning.

Other Water Policy Groups

The glass is also at least half full when it comes to land-use agency participation in other groups working on water policy. Most county governments and about half of all cities reported participation in one or more groups, with no significant difference among cities by utility type (Table 4.4). Activity is roughly evenly spread across groups dealing with groundwater, watershed, and floodplain management. Other groups include county or regional water agencies, proponents of clean water initiatives, and general water users' groups, such as countywide associations. As California grows, these issues are likely to be increasingly important for both water supply and water-quality assurance. Regional groups can facilitate resource management beyond the boundaries of individual utilities and local governments. For

Table 4.4

Land-Use Agency Participation in Other Water Policy Groups

	Cities	Counties	All
Sample size	280	35	315
Share participating (%)	54	80	57
Water policy groups (%)			
Groundwater management	23	37	24
Watershed	26	49	29
Floodplain management	20	20	20
Other	19	29	20

SOURCE: PPIC land-use planner survey.

instance, the Sacramento Water Forum, a group including city and county governments and local utilities in the Sacramento Metro region, is now aiming to coordinate land-use-based water demand projections for the next round of UWMPs.

Water Supply Adequacy Policies: A Strong Local Tradition

Somewhat to our surprise, the survey also revealed that a majority of local governments—54 percent of all cities and four out of five counties—have some form of local policy linking approval of subdivisions or permits for residential construction to water supply conditions (Table 4.5). These policies are prevalent across all regions of the state and across communities of all sizes. They generally apply to a much wider range of projects than are now required under state law; in the overwhelming majority of cases, local reviews are triggered for all new housing units.

Most local review policies were established well before the state laws requiring water adequacy (Figure 4.1). Only one-quarter of jurisdictions

Table 4.5

Local Policies Linking Approval of Subdivisions or Permits for Residential Construction to Water Supply

	No. of Jurisdictions	% Share of All Jurisdictions
Cities	152	54
Counties	29	83
Bay Area	32	53
Central Coast	23	77
Southern Coast	51	55
Inland Empire	13	48
San Joaquin Valley	18	47
Sacramento Metro	8	57
Rest of the state	36	67
California	181	57

SOURCE: PPIC land-use planner survey.
NOTE: Sample size = 315.

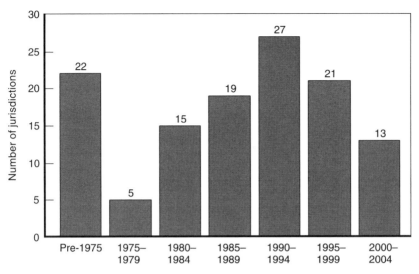

SOURCE: PPIC land-use planner survey.
NOTES: Sample size = 122. Fifty-nine jurisdictions do not indicate a starting year. The pre-1975 category includes eight jurisdictions reporting that the policy had been in place "always" or "for decades."

Figure 4.1—Year of Adoption of Local Review Policy

reporting a start date initiated their policy after 1995, the year the first state water adequacy law, SB 901, was passed. More than one-third introduced review policies during the last prolonged statewide drought, from 1987 to 1994. Despite the notoriety of water-related restrictions in some coastal communities (e.g., Santa Barbara's meter caps in the 1970s), the time profile of local policy adoption has been relatively balanced across regions.[9]

Table 4.6 summarizes planners' brief descriptions of these policies. Roughly four-fifths of agencies with local policies mentioned specific types of screening criteria or mechanisms, alone or in combination: utility oversight, adequate/available supply, conservation measures, and quantitative building caps. The remaining fifth listed more general

_____

[9]On Santa Barbara's policies, see Mercer and Morgan (1982) and Hundley (2001).

Table 4.6

Types of Local Policies Linking Water Supply and Land Use

	No. of Jurisdictions	% Share of All Jurisdictions
Specific screening policies[a]		
Require adequate/available supply	83	26
Require utility oversight		
"Will-serve" letter	34	11
Utility review	33	10
Conservation measures	7	2
Caps on new building	7	2
General policy only		
Follow general plan/specific plan/ master plan/local ordinances	17	5
Apply CEQA review	4	1
Other/unspecified	8	3

SOURCE: PPIC land-use planner survey.

NOTE: Sample size = 315.

[a]Some jurisdictions reported more than one type of policy. In all, 48 percent of the sample reported at least one specific screening policy.

policies, for instance, to "follow the general [specific] plan guidelines," to "follow the local ordinance," or to "apply CEQA guidelines."

In most cases, the policies subject new development to some form of administrative review by either the land-use authority or the utility. Nearly half of all jurisdictions with policies require that water supply be "adequate" or "available" before subdivision or permit approval.[10] If we assume that most of the general policies also entail some form of adequacy requirement, this brings the total to nearly two-thirds.

The other prevalent policy is to require direct approval by the water utility, including through the issuance of a "will-serve" letter. Utility review is much more prevalent for cities that do not have their own water department than for cities that do. It is also more prevalent in cases

---

[10]In several cases, "availability" was noted to be a function of sufficient infrastructure being in place, rather than a concern with water supply per se.

where there is less direct collaboration between land-use planners and utilities, as measured by involvement in utility planning. When land-use and water supply functions are under the same roof, utility review is more likely to be an implicit part of other policies listed. In contrast to water planning, utility type does not appear to matter for whether cities *have* a water adequacy policy, however, but only for the way the policy is carried out.

Only a handful of jurisdictions report specific conservation requirements for the approval of new development, such as retrofitting plumbing installations in existing structures or using desert landscaping on new lots. Similarly, few communities describe a local policy consisting of outright quantitative caps on new construction linked to water supply constraints.

However, water supply concerns have actually led a larger number of cities and counties across the state—13 percent in all—to use building moratoria (Table 4.7). This practice has been far more prevalent in the Central Coast and in selected unincorporated areas. Moratoria were in effect at the time of the survey in half of all cases; in most others, they were in place during drought periods in the late 1970s and from the late 1980s to the early 1990s. A quarter of Central Coast communities still have these restrictions, including large parts of unincorporated San Luis Obispo and some cities and unincorporated areas in Monterey. In the Bay Area, Napa County stands out, with several small cities in the north of the valley having extreme water restrictions. Almost all of these communities report local water adequacy screening policies (typically, adequate supplies or will-serve letters).

More generally, the prevalence of will-serve letter requirements among utility review policies deserves comment. There has been some debate over the effectiveness of such a measure, because it does not imply anything specific about the quality of the utility's own process for deciding whether water supplies are adequate for the new development. However, the survey responses give the clear impression that these are not necessarily "soft," pro forma policies. Rather, they can give utilities an opportunity to determine whether they are in a position to supply the projects—precisely the type of coordination that was missing in the Dougherty Valley case. Will-serve letter requirements are the stated

Table 4.7

Building Moratoria Resulting from Water Supply Concerns

	Ever in Effect		Currently in Effect[a]	
	Number	%	Number	%
Cities	28	10	9	3
Counties	14	40	11	31
Bay Area	8	13	3	5
Central Coast	13	43	8	27
Southern Coast	6	7	0	0
Inland Empire	3	11	0	0
San Joaquin Valley	2	5	2	5
Sacramento Metro	2	14	1	7
Rest of the state	8	15	6	11
California	42	13	20	6

NOTES: Sample size = 315. The percentages are calculated as though the 35 respondents leaving this question blank responded negatively.

[a]Excludes three jurisdictions with temporary moratoria linked to infrastructure delivery. For counties, the restrictions generally apply to specific areas, not the entire unincorporated region.

policy in a number of communities where water supply concerns are paramount, including San Luis Obispo and Santa Cruz Counties and some of the desert communities in the Coachella Valley and the Mojave Desert.

The critique of will-serve letters could, of course, apply to any of the local policies calling for review of water supply adequacy. These policies are only as good as the data upon which they are based. As the review of UWMPs shows, many utilities have important data gaps regarding long-term supply and demand planning.

Casting Safety Nets: State-Mandated Water Adequacy Screening

The recent state laws requiring water supply adequacy for new development call for review at different stages in the project approval process, albeit with broadly similar criteria.[11] SB 610 requires that jurisdictions undertake a long-term water supply assessment during a project's environmental review. It is essentially a somewhat stronger version of SB 901, passed in 1995. SB 221 requires written verification of long-term water supply by the utility that will serve the project (or, in its absence, by the city or county) at a later stage, before approval of the final subdivision map.

Both laws define "long-term" as a 20-year planning horizon, and they share a common trigger for review of residential development: more than 500 residential units or, in the case of smaller areas, projects that will increase the utility's water demand by 10 percent or more. Whereas SB 221 is focused almost exclusively on residential development, SB 610's provisions also extend to industrial and commercial developments.[12] In the interest of "smart growth" and housing affordability considerations, SB 221 exempts infill development and affordable housing from review. It also exempts jurisdictions within San Diego County deemed to be in compliance as long as the goals of the regional growth management strategy—comparable to those of the state law—are being met.

The overall similarity of the two laws, except for the timing, has led some to refer to SB 221 as the "safety net," largely superfluous unless the review done at the earlier stage is deficient. At the time of SB 221's passage, there were concerns that this net might be necessary, because experience with SB 901 had been disappointing. According to a review by SB 901's sponsor, EBMUD, only two of 119 eligible projects undergoing environmental review between 1996 and 2000 contained detailed information about long-term water supply sources.

Seen from a broader perspective, both SB 610 and SB 221 have the potential to serve as a safety net to local oversight policies. First, they can catch large projects in areas where local oversight is lacking. Second, they may increase the rigor of the local review process. Some survey

---

[11]For an overview of requirements, see Department of Water Resources (2003c).

[12]SB 610 requires review of projects that would demand an equivalent amount of water as a 500-unit residential development and other large commercial and industrial projects.

respondents acknowledged this possibility, indicating that although their utilities' word was good enough for smaller projects, they would subject these agencies to a more stringent set of documentation for projects meeting the state size threshold.

High Rates of Compliance and Stricter Review Criteria

SB 610 and SB 221 were passed amid substantially greater media fanfare than the 1995 law, and they were followed up by informational workshops co-sponsored by DWR and the CUWCC as well as outreach by the state's Building Industry Association. The survey results suggest that this publicity has paid off. In the first two years, nearly a quarter of California's local jurisdictions launched reviews under the new laws (Table 4.8).[13] An even greater number of communities expected that they would or might see review activity over the course of 2004. Not surprisingly, a higher share of counties than cities has been involved in reviews. Disproportionately high shares of total new housing as well as large projects tend to be located in unincorporated areas, where land is more readily available for development.[14]

This level of activity suggests a high degree of compliance with the new laws. To directly test this proposition, we compared the survey responses with the information on large residential projects appearing in the CEQAnet database. This database, maintained by the State Clearinghouse in the Governor's Office of Planning and Research (OPR), tracks projects undergoing CEQA review. Although CEQAnet does not cover all projects, it is likely that most large development

---

[13]The percentages of agencies with state review activity are slightly lower than those reported in Hanak and Simeti (2004). We followed up the mail survey with phone interviews in the summer of 2004, during which it was verified that some jurisdictions reporting state review activity were actually applying the local policy only. In several cases, activity was reported that occurred for the neighboring jurisdiction (e.g., a city reporting county review activity or vice versa).

[14]For instance, county planning agencies account for only 10 percent of all local land-use agencies, but they approved 22 percent of all new housing between 1996 and 2003. Whereas 41 percent of all counties approved over 500 new units in at least one year since 1996, only 24 percent of cities did so (author's calculations using data from the Construction Industry Research Board).

Table 4.8

State Reviews Under SB 610 and SB 221
(% of local jurisdictions)

	Cities	Counties	All
Launched reviews by late 2003[a]	19	43	22
Anticipate launching reviews in 2004			
Yes	19	26	19
Perhaps	25	26	25
Jurisdictions that have not already launched			
reviews but may in 2004	29	17	28

SOURCE: PPIC land-use planner survey.

NOTE: Sample size = 313 (two surveys were returned incomplete for these questions).

[a]In some cases, this can include January and February 2004.

projects are included in the database.[15] Between January 2002 and October 2003, 98 cities and counties submitted information to the State Clearinghouse on proposed residential projects meeting the 500-unit size threshold. Our survey sample is broadly representative of this group, including 61 of these 98 agencies (62%), similar to our overall survey response rate. The comparison of these two sources signals that compliance rates are good (Table 4.9). Only 13 percent of the jurisdictions with large CEQAnet projects (8 out of 61) did not report ongoing or planned SB 610/221 reviews. Three of these are within San Diego County and are potentially exempt.

Interestingly, many agencies *not* appearing in the CEQAnet list also reported review activity under the state statutes. Some of these projects met the size threshold, but others were smaller. Overall, roughly one-third of residential projects reviewed by survey respondents in 2002 and 2003 had fewer than 500 units (Table 4.10).

---

[15]Local agencies are required to report CEQA-eligible projects to OPR only when a state agency needs to be involved in project review or permitting, which is most likely for larger development projects.

Table 4.9

SB 610 and SB 221 Compliance: A Comparison of Survey Results and CEQAnet

State Review Status	Jurisdictions with CEQAnet Projects[a]	Other Jurisdictions	Total
Launched in 2000–2003	43	26	69
Will launch in 2004	6	23	29
May launch in 2004	4	55	59
No state review planned	8	148	156
Total	61	252	313

SOURCE: PPIC land-use planner survey and CEQAnet database.

[a]Residential projects ≥ 499 units reported to the CEQAnet database between January 2002 and October 2003.

Table 4.10

Size of Projects Reviewed Under SB 610 and SB 221

	Jurisdictions	Projects
Residential/mixed use		
Fewer than 10 units	2	6
10–99 units	3	4
100–399 units	9	11
400–499 units	7	8
500 or more units	45	65
Other[a]	2	3
Commercial/industrial	13	18

SOURCE: PPIC land-use planner survey.

NOTE: Sample size = 313.

[a]Includes residential projects with other size indicators (e.g., acres).

A Significant Safety Net

It would be tempting to conclude that this pattern of greater stringency stems from stricter local water adequacy policies in communities for which the state laws are superfluous. However, jurisdictions *without* local policies were actually twice as likely to report state reviews for smaller projects. Thus, in practice, the mesh on the safety net appears tighter than called for by the letter of the law.

But just how big is the net? In other words, how many communities without local oversight policies are being spurred into action by the presence of the new state laws? Although SB 610/221 review activity is highest in the communities that also have local policies, this safety net role is significant (Table 4.11). Within the first two years, one-third of jurisdictions conducting these reviews (or 7% of the sample) fell into this category. If we include those anticipating some review activity in 2004, the state laws will already have served as the safety net in nearly 20 percent of all local jurisdictions within the first three years.

Across regions, the safety net is most important in the fast-growing Inland Empire and San Joaquin Valley, catching projects in over a third of all communities (Figure 4.2). It is there and in the Sacramento Metro region that the new laws have also had the most pronounced stimulus effect, spurring the adoption of local policies.[16] As an example,

Table 4.11

Local and State Review Activity
(% of jurisdictions)

	Local Policy	No Local Policy
State reviews by end of 2003	15	7
Additional jurisdictions that may launch reviews in 2004	16	13
No state reviews done or foreseen	27	23

SOURCE: PPIC land-use planner survey.

NOTE: Sample size = 313.

---

[16]Of the eight local policies adopted since 2002, five were in the Inland Empire or the San Joaquin Valley, one in Sacramento, and two in Sutter County, a fast-growing rural county bordering the Sacramento Metro region.

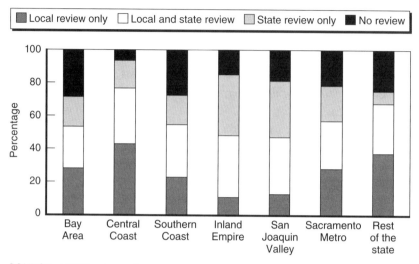

SOURCE: PPIC land-use planner survey.
NOTES: Sample size = 313. The categories with state review activity include jurisdictions that said they would or might conduct reviews in 2004.

Figure 4.2—Regional Patterns of Water Adequacy Review Activity

Riverside County, for years one of the state's largest issuers of residential building permits, adopted a policy in 2003 to facilitate review of projects deemed significant, even if they fall below the 500-unit threshold.

Among the quarter of the state's communities reporting neither state nor local review procedures for water supply adequacy, many may have little need for it. As a group, they have experienced significantly lower housing growth since the mid-1990s; in survey remarks, one-quarter indicated that they were either built-out or facing no growth pressure. No region has more than 30 percent of its communities in this "no review" category. Coverage by local or state policies is almost universal in the Central Coast, where water supply concerns continue to be a fact of daily life for local planners, developers, and sometimes even residents wishing to add bathrooms to their homes.

Summing Up

In California and elsewhere in the West, there has been concern over the potential negative consequences of the institutional split between utilities, responsible for water supply, and local governments, responsible for the land-use decisions that affect water demand. Our survey of city and county land-use planners suggests that this disconnect is not as big as many might have imagined or feared. In six out of 10 cases, land-use agencies participate in the planning activities of at least some of their local utilities. Nearly as often, they are active in other water policy groups concerned with regional resource management issues. Direct collaboration with utilities is highest in cities that have their own water departments, suggesting that formal institutional linkages between water and land-use agencies enhance contact and information sharing. Given the evidence that the quality of utility plans benefits from this collaboration, special efforts may be needed to enhance coordination when utilities are distinct entities, including special districts and private companies.

A central concern has been that the local government-utility disconnect will lead to the approval of new development in spite of inadequate water supplies, putting existing residents and new homebuyers at risk of shortages. We find that over half of all cities and most counties have some form of local oversight policy to guard against this possibility. Moreover, cities without their own water departments do just as well as those with in-house utilities on this score; they simply rely more heavily on outside review by their utilities for this assessment.

SB 610 and SB 221, the new state laws requiring review of long-term supplies for large developments, are nevertheless playing an important safety net function, catching projects that would otherwise fall through the cracks because of an absence of local oversight. Within the first three years, nearly 20 percent of local governments without their own policies expected to conduct reviews under the new laws. State review activity is also high for jurisdictions with their own policies, and overall compliance appears good.

The evidence also suggests that local governments are casting a more finely meshed net than required by the law, reviewing many projects below the 500-unit threshold. Some observers have raised concerns about the quality of the water adequacy assessments, however. The downside risks of weak assessments are twofold. If utilities and local governments are overly optimistic about supply capabilities, the original intent of the policies is thwarted, and communities are put at risk of water shortages. But if they err on the side of caution, they are likely to block the development of new housing, a sorely needed commodity in a growing state. How well California's communities are faring in this regard is the subject of the next chapter.

5. Is Water Policy Affecting Housing Growth?

In the debates surrounding the passage of the state's new "show me the water" laws, both sides expressed concerns about the review process for determining adequate supplies. While proponents of the legislation worried that the laws were too lenient, cities, counties, water agencies, and builders expressed apprehension about the laws' potential to engage them in a spate of frivolous lawsuits and to unreasonably block development.[1]

At the heart of these debates are the standards for determining whether long-term supplies are sufficient to support new development. Although the laws leave the amount of water needed to support a new project to the discretion of the reviewing agency, they do provide some guidance on evaluating supply sufficiency. Under the provisions of SB 610, a water supply assessment must consider reliability in the face of a multiyear drought, and agencies conducting the review are required to consider "real" water supplies, not just the amounts listed in contracts and water-rights decrees. Significantly, state law does not require that communities make water available for growth, either by developing new supply sources or by freeing up existing supplies through conservation.

Supply reliability is open to interpretation, particularly when the underlying data are uncertain or in dispute. As a consequence, there is a potential for reviews to gloss over potential problems or to state an overly conservative view of available supplies. These same issues arise for reviews under local water adequacy screening policies.

Without detailed information on the quality of each review, it is difficult to evaluate the extent to which they may be erring on the side of imprudence or caution. An alternative is to examine outcomes in terms

---

[1] For a detailed account of the negotiation process leading up to the passage of SB 610 and SB 221, see Association of California Water Agencies (2002).

of water availability and housing growth. But this approach also has limitations. To date, the few cases where water shortages have been linked to excessive development are in outlying areas relying on limited groundwater resources or small lakes.[2] In larger systems, the water supply consequences of an inadequate review may not be seen for years or even decades.

It is possible to assess the influence of screening on housing growth, but this still begs the question of whether a slowdown is reasonable or excessive. If water adequacy screening does deter growth, this may reflect responsible management of a limited supply. But there is also a clear potential for screening to be used as a tool to limit growth, irrespective of water supply options available to the community. The most obvious cases are when communities reject water supply development options to prevent new growth from occurring. This could include refusal to adopt conservation policies that could free up supplies for new residents.

With these caveats in mind, this chapter examines the effects of water adequacy reviews on the approval of new development in California. We begin with a discussion of the experience in implementing the new state laws: Are reviews influencing projects' size or footprint? How contentious is the process proving to be? We then evaluate the quantitative effects of screening on housing growth. This analysis focuses on the role of local policies, which have been in place longer. As an indirect test of whether communities are using these policies to slow growth, we then examine the record on water conservation. Are communities that screen for water availability providing evidence of good stewardship over water resources more generally?

State-Mandated Reviews: Globally Positive, with Some Battle Scars

As our survey results show, the new state laws have generated a considerable amount of review activity. To develop a picture of how

---

[2]This issue has recently come up in the Shaver Lake area in the foothills of Fresno County, which relies on wells overlying fractured rock, a limited source with little or no recharge potential (Benjamin, 2004).

implementation was proceeding, we conducted follow-up phone interviews in the summer of 2004 with planners in 59 cities and counties across the state that reported review activity in the mail survey.[3] By that time, water adequacy reviews (mostly under SB 610, in some cases under both laws) had been completed for 95 projects, and were under way or about to be launched for another 19.

The story that emerges is, in our view, a very balanced one. The vast majority of projects—86 out of 95—were deemed to have sufficient supplies. Of the remaining nine, the only two that were definitively rejected had counted on uncertain groundwater supplies in outlying areas. One 1,048-unit project had sought to locate in a desert area over which San Diego County has long exercised strict regulatory control because of the basin's limited recharge capabilities. The second was a very small project in an outlying area of Solano County.

Drawing Boards and Footprints

The other seven projects deemed insufficient were sent back to the drawing board to find alternative sources. Three of these, encompassing nearly 2,000 homes, a hospital complex, and an industrial laboratory, were proposed in Redwood City (San Mateo County). Because the municipal utility has been overdrawing its surface water allotments, the city conditioned new development on the introduction of recycled water for a range of outdoor uses, both on- and off-project. Following over a year of contentious public debates, the city council approved the recycling plan in early 2004, paving the way for the projects to go forward. Three other residential projects—2,200 units in unincorporated Placer County, 1,000 units in Beaumont (Riverside County), and 155 units in Glendora (Los Angeles County)—may be required to bring in additional surface water or to scale back. In the seventh case, the city of Modesto chose not to annex and serve a 1,200-unit project in unincorporated Stanislaus County, which is now forming a water district to serve it with treated groundwater.

For projects deemed to have sufficient supplies, the approval process appears to have been taken quite seriously. In several cases, developers

---

[3]We were unable to reach nine jurisdictions that reported review activity.

purchased water from other agencies to augment local supplies. In several others, they were required to finance the local utility's own supply expansion projects through impact fees.

Perhaps most striking is the attention devoted to recycling and conservation. Three out of 10 approved projects are planning to use recycled or raw water for landscaping, adopt landscape conservation strategies, and/or augment indoor conservation with water-saving appliances and retrofits in existing neighborhoods.[4] In some cases, these components were incorporated into project design before review; in others, they have been added as a condition of approval. This experience suggests that the new state laws will help foster the use of recycled water, still an underexploited resource in California, and possibly alter the footprint of development by reducing outdoor water use in new neighborhoods.

In general, local governments appear to be applying more stringent standards for water supply adequacy, expecting permanent sources to back new growth, rather than the 20-year supply required by statute.

Local Controversy: Is It About Water, or Is It About Growth?

On the whole, the review process appears to have proceeded without widespread controversy. Yet there are some notable exceptions. In these cases, it can be difficult to disentangle whether the controversy stems from legitimate concerns over water supplies or from a hidden agenda to slow growth.

The Redwood City case mentioned above generated public concern over the potential health risks of using recycled water on lawns and playing fields in neighborhoods currently using drinking-quality water for these purposes. In response, the plan was modified to restrict recycled water to areas where children do not play and to introduce artificial turf on some playing fields. The citizens' group then dropped its opposition, suggesting that its primary concern was indeed with water issues.

---

[4]Another tenth of the sample is planning to incorporate outdoor conservation policies consistent with general local policies.

The situation is more ambiguous in several cases where citizens' groups have objected to augmenting supplies to support new development. The insufficient supply determination in the Beaumont project arose in the context of opposition by a grassroots citizen's group. Initially, the group filed suit against the developer on grounds that the project was backed by insufficient water supplies. Following a judge's ruling in the group's favor, the project EIR was revised to include water from a new transfer the city arranged with a neighboring utility. The group then filed a suit over the transfer, arguing that it should all be used for basin recharge rather than for development (Moore, 2004a). It has succeeded in holding up the transfer on procedural grounds, with a court ruling that the transfer itself must be subject to a full environmental review before proceeding—a step now under way (Moore, 2004b).

A similar controversy has arisen in the city of Tracy, located in a fast-growing area in western San Joaquin County. The municipal water department has been purchasing agricultural water from local irrigation districts to boost local supplies, and it requires that developers of very large projects do the same. Local environmental groups have launched lawsuits against several of these transactions, on grounds that they encourage the development of agricultural land and urban sprawl. One suit was settled with an agreement to provide some environmental mitigation. A second was rejected in trial court and is now on appeal but has been allowed to stand in the meantime. In November 2003, Tracy residents approved the halving of growth caps, putting some of the proposed development projects on hold.

Water and Growth in the Santa Clarita Valley

California's most prominent recent controversy over water and growth issues also involves water transfers. The development of land owned by the Newhall Corporation, in unincorporated Los Angeles County, has generated numerous lawsuits against the developer, local water agencies, and the county. Local citizens' groups have challenged the water supply sources for the 22,000-unit Newhall Ranch project and the 2,500-unit West Creek project as well as the water supply analysis in the local Urban Water Management Plan.

Initially, the Newhall Ranch project intended to use water from a large, permanent transfer of State Water Project (SWP) water from the Kern County Water Agency (KCWA) to the Castaic Lake Water Agency (CLWA), the regional wholesaler. Local groups objected both to the transfer and its use for the project, arguing that it was "paper water," not a reliable source for development. In 2000, a judge overturned Los Angeles County's approval of the project, ordering officials to reconsider the effects on water and other issues.[5] Rather than waiting for the legal battle to be resolved on the KCWA-CLWA transfer, Newhall released a revised EIR in December 2002 with alternative water sources, including a permanent transfer of water from a private party in Kern County, based on more reliable water rights. The local groups objected to this transfer because of its private provenance but did not challenge its legality, and the court approved the final EIR for the Newhall Ranch project in October 2003 (Ricardi and Fausset, 2002; Fausset, 2003).

The EIR for the West Creek project also relied on water from the pending KCWA transfer to CLWA. The local opponents argued, again, that the water supply analysis was inadequate, because it failed to consider the reliability of supplies from SWP sources. This case came to court in 2002, following the enactment of the new state laws. In the final EIR, Newhall argued that the absence of detailed information on adequate supplies in the environmental review stage (SB 610) would be remedied before final subdivision map approval under the requirements of SB 221. In February 2003, an appellate court rejected this argument, sending Newhall back to the drawing board to provide substantial evidence of water availability, including in drought periods, as required by SB 610.[6]

These two challenges related largely to the reliability of SWP water to support new development, as reported in project EIRs prepared by the developer. In 2001, a court battle was launched against CLWA and its four retail agencies on grounds that their joint UWMP did not

[5]Ventura County was also party to this suit, objecting to the project's traffic and open space implications. These issues as well as wildlife protection concerns were mitigated in the final project EIR, and Ventura County dropped its lawsuit.

[6]*Santa Clarita Organization for Planning the Environment v. County of Los Angeles*, 106 Cal. App. 4th 715 (2003, 2nd Dist.).

adequately address the reliability of the region's other major water source—local groundwater. Perchlorate contamination had been detected in 1997, and the UWMP, while noting the problem, did not provide a detailed remediation plan. In September 2004, an appellate court ruled that a UWMP lacking a reliable analysis of the availability of water is "fatally flawed" and instructed the trial court to invalidate the water agencies' approval of their UWMP.[7] In an effort to comply with the ruling, CLWA's board adopted an updated version of its 2000 UWMP in January 2005.

The citizens' group challenges of the project EIRs and the UWMP have helped demonstrate that the state water and land-use planning laws have teeth. The rulings put developers, land-use authorities, and utilities on notice that planning documents can be successfully challenged if they do not provide adequate analysis of long-term water availability, including reliability in dry years. As such, these outcomes clearly support the intent of the laws—to avoid water shortages through sound water and land-use planning.

Nevertheless, some of the actions undertaken by the local challengers suggest that they have been motivated not just by water supply concerns but also by a desire to slow growth. In particular, lawsuits against water transfers—a way to make new water available—have been an important part of the overall strategy. A suit was filed in 2000 against the permanent transfer of KCWA water to CLWA. In the fall of 2002, CLWA also had the opportunity to purchase temporary surplus SWP water and store it in a Kern County groundwater bank. The local groups challenged this transfer, too, arguing that it would be used for growth (Fausset, 2002). The courts have allowed both transfers to stand.[8] In January 2005, however, two statewide environmental groups filed suit

---

[7] *Friends of Santa Clara River v. Castaic Lake Water Agency*, 123 Cal. App. 4th 1 (2004, 5th Dist.).

[8] In the case of the permanent transfer, an appellate court ruling sided with the plaintiffs on a procedural matter and instructed the EIR for the transfer to be rewritten to reflect subsequent developments regarding a related State Water Project EIR (*Friends of Santa Clara River v. Castaic Lake Water Agency*, 95 Cal. App 4th 1373). The transfer was allowed to stand pending this revision.

against the permanent transfer, potentially reopening the question of its validity (Alanez, 2005).

The Groundwater Problem

The lawsuit against Castaic Lake's UWMP focused on the reliability of groundwater supplies, given the potential costs of restoring water quality to acceptable levels. Elsewhere, the development approval process is coming up against problems linked to the availability of supplies and who should have access to them. At the heart of these problems is the issue of basin management. As noted above, groundwater basins are subject to strict management protocols in only a limited number of places in California, including parts of Southern California and some coastal areas farther to the north. In adjudicated basins, overall withdrawal rights are apportioned among users, and the water master monitors basin health and recommends adjustments as needed. In special districts, the management entity organizes recharge activity and charges water users a pump fee based on replacement costs.

Elsewhere, information on the basin is often less developed, and rules are less clear concerning the overall "safe yield" levels of withdrawals and how these volumes should be apportioned among users.[9] Our phone survey revealed two areas where conflicts have erupted over the use of unmanaged groundwater supplies to support large projects. In San Luis Obispo County, the central issue is reliability of data on basin capacity. The environmental review for the 1,300-unit Woodlands project concluded that adequate supplies existed to support its reliance on well water. Following an outside review of this basin study and another, less optimistic, study by DWR, the county planning department recommended that the board of supervisors adopt stricter growth controls for groundwater-based development. This position was also supported by a water district neighboring the Woodlands site, concerned about the project's effects on its wells. The board of supervisors instead recommended a water supply determination requiring more conservation, and the Woodlands project has been allowed to go forward.

---

[9]See Department of Water Resources (2003d) and Hanak (2003).

In Kern County, where information on basin characteristics is probably better, the issue has centered on use-rights. The county's first SB 610 review was for the 1,200-unit Copa de Oro project, for which the developer planned to use water from an unadjudicated basin. Although the review determined that supplies were adequate, a neighboring water district expressed concern about overdraft, and the project was revised to include conservation measures and recycled water. The developer also agreed to monitor all wells and share the data with the water district. As a result of this experience, the County's General Plan update now requires that high water users show supplies in addition to groundwater. However, a new controversy is already brewing over two planned projects that have designs on the same groundwater reserves in another part of the county.

Similar issues have been raised in some areas of inland Southern California where basins are not yet fully managed, including the Antelope Valley in eastern Los Angeles County and the Coachella Valley in Riverside County. The development of sound information on basin capacity and workable protocols for sustainable groundwater use is a major challenge in fast-growing areas of the state, to which we return in the next chapter.

Housing Market Effects of Water Adequacy Screening

The record to date suggests that the new state laws may lead to a slowdown in housing growth in some areas. Although few projects have been rejected outright, others may be downsized, and still others may take longer to gain final approval, given conflicts over water supply sources and the attendant legal battles. However, it is premature to provide a quantitative assessment of these effects, because most projects reviewed under these laws have not yet made it through the pipeline to permitting and construction. For this reason, we propose to examine the housing market effects of regulation by focusing on the role of the local water adequacy screening policies, which have a longer history.

A Framework for Analysis

From the standpoint of the housing market, it is appropriate to consider measures to screen for water supply adequacy as a form of growth management or growth control. The general growth control toolkit contains a variety of measures. Zoning, urban growth boundaries, and growth caps are explicit quantity-based tools to regulate development within an area. Impact fees are a common price-based tool, used to exact up-front contributions to the cost of increasing local public service capacity. The economics literature on housing markets predicts that growth controls of various types will slow housing growth.

Requiring screening for water adequacy is most akin to a quantitative growth control measure known as an Adequate Public Facilities Ordinance or APFO. APFOs require the availability of service infrastructure (typically for water and wastewater) before approval of construction. The key distinction between water adequacy screening requirements and APFOs is that the former is concerned with the overall *supply* of water available to users in the area, whereas the latter is concerned with the availability of the *hardware* (pipes and treatment facilities) for water and wastewater delivery.

In some western states, localities systematically charge separate impact fees for these two components of the water system: a "raw water" or "water resources" fee is levied to enable the local utility to acquire additional supplies, and a "connection" or "system expansion" fee contributes to the local infrastructure. In Colorado's fast-growing Front Range, for instance, raw water fees are typically in the range of $5,000 to $7,000 per home, and total water impact fees are several thousand dollars higher.

In California, connection fees have been widely used for at least a decade, and they are still relatively low, averaging just under $2,200 per home in 2003. Few communities have explicit up-front payment requirements for the acquisition of new supplies, however. Instead, water adequacy screening generally functions as a layer of review, with the potential for case-by-case negotiations with developers on specific solutions.

Although explicit meter caps are rare, one might expect jurisdictions with water adequacy screening policies to take longer to approve development than places that do not have this layer of review. Projects may also be downsized through this process. To assess whether water adequacy screening is slowing residential construction in California, we estimated a model of housing supply, taking into account market conditions and other growth-related policies.[10] In particular, we wanted to ascertain that the local screening policies are not simply measuring a community's general predilection to control growth. Fortunately, we were able to control for this by including measures of general growth control policies from two previous studies.

We also sought to measure the effects of water impact fees. Although such fees are considered a growth management tool, with the potential to dampen housing growth, they may have some advantages in relation to quantity controls and ad hoc reviews. In particular, the presence of a known fee may take some uncertainty and delay out of the development process for builders. Assessing the effects of impact fees is of interest, given their potential role in making new water available to communities. Water connection fees are used in about three-quarters of the jurisdictions in our sample.

Data on general growth management measures and fees are on hand for only portions of the jurisdictions for which we have basic data on new housing, water adequacy policies, and market conditions. To include as many jurisdictions as possible, we therefore conducted the analysis over several different samples. The results reported below present the range of estimates for these samples.

Screening Policies Have Slowed Growth Since the Mid-1990s

Since 1994, the point at which California's housing market began to emerge from a multiyear slump, water adequacy screening policies have significantly slowed issuance of permits for residential construction. This effect is unambiguous for the roughly 10 percent of jurisdictions that adopted new policies after that year. But growth also appears to have been slower in those cities and counties that adopted screening policies earlier, suggesting that the housing market effects of these policies are persistent. We estimate that, between 1994 and 2003, on average, cities

---

[10]For a detailed discussion of the model, data, and results, see Appendix C.

and counties with water adequacy screening policies issued 13 to 22 percent fewer residential construction permits than did jurisdictions without these policies. For some subgroups of cities, this effect is even stronger. Although these effects may appear large, they are in line with the findings of a national study of the housing supply effects of growth controls in metropolitan areas (Mayer and Somerville, 2000a). That study found that each additional month of delay in the issuance of building permits reduced growth by 10 to 12 percent and that each new growth control measure led to a 7 percent decline.

Because local screening policies are so prevalent in California— present in over half of all jurisdictions by 2003—the net outcome on the state's housing market is potentially quite substantial. Since 1994, the implied decrease in new housing supply has been in the range of 7 to 12 percent. If some developers shifted to jurisdictions without screening policies, where permits are easier to obtain, this would have dampened the aggregate effect on the housing market.

These estimated effects of water adequacy screening policies are distinct from any effects that general growth control policies might have on housing. Indeed, in contrast to the water policies, the general measures of growth controls are positively associated with new housing, reflecting the fact that communities facing the most growth pressure are more likely to adopt them. It is not possible to see whether these general measures slow the subsequent pace of growth, because we do not have information on when they were adopted.[11]

Water Impact Fees Have Not Slowed Growth

Growing communities use water connection fees to help cover the costs of expanding service provision, but the adoption of fees does not appear to slow growth. Nor have increases in fee levels generated negative effects on housing over the period under review. These results suggest that communities restricting growth because of limited water supplies would do well to consider charging higher up-front fees to help

---

[11]For alternative frameworks analyzing the housing market effects of general growth controls in California, see Levine (1999), Lewis and Neiman (2002), and Quigley and Raphael (2004). Although Quigley and Raphael provide evidence that these controls raise prices, the effects on housing supply are less clear.

pay for new water. Because water fees are still low in California, it is of course possible that raising fees more systematically could slow housing in the future. However, evidence from Colorado, where fees are higher both in absolute terms and as a share of median home prices, also suggests that fee increases do not slow growth (Hanak and Chen, 2005).

Conservation: A Litmus Test for Responsible Resource Management

If communities are truly resource-constrained, the slowing of growth in line with water availability may be an appropriate outcome. However, as we have seen, there is a considerable margin for water savings through conservation in California. Although the "beneficial use" doctrine that guides legal rights to water use does not mandate communities to conserve, there is a growing presumption that conservation is part of a socially responsible water management policy. It is important to ask whether jurisdictions that adopt water adequacy policies are implementing such measures. If not, the screening policies may enable local users to hoard a resource over which they happen to enjoy the use-rights of first-comers. Whether or not this is the intention of water adequacy screening policies, it is an outcome that should raise concerns, given the unrealized potential for cost-effective conservation, the environmental costs associated with many other new water supply alternatives, and the challenge of housing affordability in California.

Jurisdictions with Water Adequacy Screening Policies Are Not Better Stewards

As a first pass in this analysis, we examine the average rates of adoption of conservation-oriented rate structures (increasing block rate or seasonal pricing) and other Best Management Practices for jurisdictions with and without water adequacy screening policies (Table 5.1). For the BMPs, the sample is restricted to utilities that are required to submit reports to the CUWCC. This includes CUWCC members—more heavily concentrated in coastal areas—and municipal contractors to the Central Valley Project. The data reveal considerable differences in adoption rates across BMPs, ranging from under 40 percent for

Table 5.1

Adoption of Conservation Measures by Jurisdictions With and Without Water Adequacy Screening Policies (% of jurisdictions)

	Has Screening Policy	Does Not Have Screening Policy
Rate structure (BMP 11)		
Increasing block rates or summer rates	44	45
Uniform rate	42	45
Unmetered rate	14	10
Number of observations	97	135
Other conservation measures		
BMP 1: Strategy for single-family residential water-use surveys	64	76
BMP 2: High-flow showerhead replacement ordinance	37	33
Strategy for distributing low-flow showerheads	81	82
BMP 3: Prescreening system audit	40	39
BMP 4: Meters for new connections and billing by volume	99	98
BMP 5: Strategy for landscape surveys	56	59
BMP 6: Energy, water, or wastewater utility rebates for high-efficiency washing machines	81	76
BMP 7: Active public information program on conservation	98	95
BMP 8: School information programs	97	91
BMP 9: Commercial customers ranked by use	75	78
Industrial customers ranked by use	74	76
Institutional customers ranked by use	73	78
BMP 12: Conservation coordinator	96	95
BMP 13: Water waste prohibition ordinance	74	79
BMP 14: Ultra-low flush toilet replacement for single-family units	78	74
Ultra-low flush toilet replacement for multifamily units	76	73
Number of observations	53	66

SOURCES: Rate structure, Black and Veatch (2003); other measures, CUWCC (www.cuwcc.org).

NOTES: The table reports the percentage of jurisdictions that have adopted the listed policy. For jurisdictions with multiple utilities, the mean adoption rate was used. Rate structures are for 2003. BMPs are generally for 2002, but data for preceding years were used if they were missing for that year. BMP 10 was excluded because it applies only to wholesale utilities. The number of observations varies slightly for some of the BMPs. For all variables, ANOVA tests rejected the hypothesis that the mean values for jurisdictions with and without water adequacy screening policies were different.

ordinances requiring replacement of high-flow showerheads (a component of BMP 2) to nearly 100 percent for employing a conservation coordinator (BMP 12). However, these simple comparisons reveal no significant differences in adoption rates between jurisdictions with and without water adequacy screening policies, for any conservation measure.

Because utilities make the decision to adopt many of these measures, adoption patterns may not fully reflect the desires of the local governments. Local governments with their own municipal water departments should have more flexibility to choose conservation policies, because they directly control utility policy. We therefore conducted a more detailed analysis of the adoption of increasing block rate and peak rate pricing policies, controlling for utility type and some other factors that might be expected to influence adoption.[12] Notably, these models include service area population as a measure of size, because larger utilities may have a technical advantage in switching to these more sophisticated rates. They also control for average summer temperature, because the water conservation advantages of conservation rate structures are greatest in hotter climates, where landscaping uses are higher.

The analysis confirms the absence of a relationship between local water adequacy screening policies and the use of tiered or peak-rate pricing. Moreover, there is no evidence that the subset of jurisdictions with their own water departments is more likely to adopt these rate structures. Factors that do make a difference are size, which exhibits the predicted positive relationship to conservation pricing, and utility type. Private utilities are substantially less likely than special districts to adopt these rate structures, and city departments may also be less likely to do so.

From the standpoint of water conservation, it is troubling to find that utilities in hotter areas are actually *less* likely to use conservation-oriented rate structures to moderate water use. We saw evidence of this problem when we examined the regional patterns of rate structures in Chapter 2. This analysis confirms that the lower rates of conservation

---

[12]For details, see Appendix D.

pricing in the state's inland areas are not due to technical handicaps related to utility size.

A Problem of Water-Rights Law?

The absence of a clear association between water adequacy screening policies and conservation practices lends credence to the view that screening is being used in some communities as a tool for limiting growth, not as a tool for resource planning. In this sense, a failure to adopt conservation policies can be likened to the actions described above, where some citizens' groups have sought to prevent the development of new water sources to block growth. As with water transfers, conservation has been an explicit pawn in some growth debates.

Perhaps the most extreme example occurred in Sacramento County, when the city of Folsom was attempting to introduce meters in 2002. An antigrowth citizen's group ran a campaign against metering, arguing that the water saved would be used to accommodate new development (Hecht, 2001). Residents rejected the switch to metering, putting the city in a position of facing serious sanctions from its main supplier, the Central Valley Project. Since then, the citizen's group has been attempting to gain voter support of general growth controls (Vellinga, 2004).

The public perception that conservation is undesirable—because it will just pave the way for more growth—is one that numerous local officials acknowledge. In professional meetings discussing the adoption of conservation rate structures and related policies, public unease over the potential links to more growth is one of the main obstacles cited. Existing residents appear much more willing to let newcomers undertake conservation—for instance, by imposing stricter water-use provisions on new development—than they are to impose it on themselves.

This situation stems from the nature of water-rights laws in California, in which communities hold long-standing rights to the use of specific water sources. Beyond some federal and state regulations concerning the use of low-flow indoor plumbing devices in new homes, communities are largely free to determine what constitutes appropriate use. In contrast to a resource such as fuel, there is no automatic pricing mechanism to encourage conservation as growth puts pressure on water resources statewide.

Communities with access to ample, low-cost supplies may actually benefit by maintaining this advantage, because it enhances their amenities relative to places where water is in shorter supply. However, this policy is clearly questionable at the level of society at large. Newcomers and renters bear all the costs of scarcity (including the rise in home prices resulting from a slowdown in new construction), while existing property owners amass capital gains from water rights developed decades earlier.

Breaking this cycle may require a combination of carrots and sticks. Carrots are financial incentives to help cover the costs of implementing conservation policies. For instance, several California utilities have embarked on a policy of "conservation offsets" to make water available for growth, with investments in water-efficient retrofits financed by state grants and impact fees. Over the past few years, the Southern Nevada Water Authority (SNWA), wholesaler to the Las Vegas Valley, has made major inroads on outdoor water use with a turf buy-back program financed by impact fees. Following a price increase from $0.40 to $1 per square foot of turf converted, the agency "purchased" nearly 2,000 acres of turf during 2003 and 2004, generating a net water savings of roughly 15,000 acre-feet.[13] Participants are required to replace the turf with mulch and at least 50 percent plant cover and to maintain a low-water-using landscape for at least 10 years. According to the SNWA, the program is changing attitudes about what looks good in a desert climate; reduced lawn maintenance during the hot Las Vegas summers is also a big draw.

The harsh climate actually makes Las Vegas an easy testing site, because the water savings are so high (55 to 62 gallons per ft^2). Utilities in milder climates—including most California locations—would generally need to pay less, even though participants' costs of replacing landscapes (an estimated $2 per ft^2) are not likely to be lower. Several

---

[13]Data on the program were provided by Tracy Bower, Southern Nevada Water Authority, February 6, 2005. For more details on program requirements, see the SNWA website: www.snwa.com.

California utilities have experimented with lower-fee variations on this theme (including the North Marin Water District's "cash for grass" program, instituted during the early 1990s drought). Within its large service area, MWDSC has instead been promoting low-water-using landscaping options through a public education campaign, in which it has attempted to enlist both builders and garden supply chains. The recently launched Landscape Task Force, facilitated by the CUWCC, is examining the scope for encouraging attractive, water-efficient landscaping options statewide.

Sticks include regulations to foster conservation. These can include new standards for appliances, such as the new requirement to purchase water-efficient washing machines starting in 2007. Another example is the policy, finally passed into California law in the fall of 2004, to require that all municipal utilities switch to metered rates by 2025. Landscaping ordinances, which restrict the amount of turf that can be planted on new properties, are still rare in California, but they are now commonplace both in Las Vegas and in Arizona. Policies such as these refine the definition of beneficial use. Given the absence of clear market-based incentives for communities to conserve, regulations that help shape the notion of what uses are acceptable may be a necessary part of the policy portfolio.

Summing Up

The early experience under the new state "show me the water" laws should assuage the worst fears on both sides of the water and growth debates. The new review process is not generating a flood of lawsuits against developers and water agencies. Nor is it systematically glossing over water supply problems to push ahead with new projects. In various places, developers are being sent back to the drawing board to come up with more secure supply options, and many projects are being designed to incorporate recycling and conservation measures. Projects are typically backed by permanent supplies, not just 20 years' worth.

The lawsuits that have been filed do tend to be linked to local controversies about the desirability of growth per se, not just to water supply concerns. A telltale sign is that citizens' groups have not only challenged the quality of water supply assessments; they have also opposed augmenting supplies to support new development. These controversies have nevertheless proven a useful testing ground for the enforceability of the state laws. Appellate court rulings concerning the Santa Clarita Valley have put developers, land-use authorities, and utilities on notice that both project water supply assessments and UWMPs can be successfully challenged if they do not adequately analyze long-term supply reliability.

In areas with unmanaged groundwater basins, we should expect to see more lawsuits on the horizon. To avoid unsustainable pumping, there is a need to develop better information on supplies and workable rules on use-rights. Unless current and potential users can work out management agreements on their own, the courts may be the most appropriate venue for apportioning groundwater for growth. Without better basin management, fast-growing, groundwater-dependent areas including much of the San Joaquin Valley risk aquifer depletion and the range of adverse consequences it brings.

Because screening for water adequacy adds a layer of review to the development approval process, it may delay approvals and result in project downsizing, thereby slowing the pace of residential construction. Our analysis of California housing supply, factoring in local screening policies and other growth controls, confirms this slowdown. Since 1994, jurisdictions with screening policies have curtailed issuance of new housing permits by 13 to 22 percent, with even greater declines in urban areas. This is clearly of potential concern in a state that ranks poorly in both housing affordability and homeownership.

If a construction slowdown is really needed to protect existing residents from water shortages, then this outcome could be taken as a sign of good planning and good stewardship. However, communities that screen for water are not doing any better than their neighbors by another yardstick of good stewardship—conservation. Instead, some communities have chosen to restrict development while maintaining access to high levels of low-cost water.

California law does not mandate communities to make water available for development, through conservation or any other means. But if we are to accommodate the millions of new residents anticipated over the coming decades, new water will need to be part of the equation.

As we saw in Chapter 2, studies have shown that urban conservation is one of the largest potential sources of cost-effective new supplies. The implication is clear: Conservation by existing residents will need to be part of the new water portfolio.

6. Meeting the Water Supply Challenges of Growth

In conclusion, the message emerging from this review of water and growth issues in California is one of cautious optimism. With a portfolio approach, guided by the dual principles of cost-effectiveness and respect for the environment, there are ample opportunities to find water to accommodate anticipated growth over the decades to come. This portfolio is diverse; groundwater banking, recycling, and water transfers are each likely to play at least as big a role as the more traditional option of expanding surface storage. One of the largest potential reservoirs is urban conservation.

There would be fewer grounds for optimism if all we had were the simple calculations showing that supply could potentially equal demand. Today, just about every new supply option faces at least some institutional hurdles, whether to gain public acceptance or to meet environmental approvals. But progress is being made on various fronts to overcome these hurdles. Successful models already exist for using recycled water for urban landscaping, for protecting neighbors from the potential negative effects of groundwater banking, and for using conservation-oriented rate structures. Projects now under way will provide guidance on the use of recycled water for basin recharge, on workable methods for mitigating third-party effects of water transfers, and on the management of brine from desalination facilities. Most of this experimentation is taking place at the initiative of local and regional utilities, as part of their efforts to meet local water demands.

In California, both water supply and land-use planning are local responsibilities, in the hands of hundreds of utilities and city and county governments. Our analysis of local entities' planning and coordinating activities also suggests some grounds for optimism. Municipal utilities have come a long way since the mid-1980s, when the first Urban Water

Management Plans were due. In the 2000-round, long-term planning documents were submitted by the vast majority of eligible agencies, serving over three-quarters of the state's population. These plans still have some important gaps, but it is not a stretch to say that the glass is at least half full for local water planning.

Similarly, the evidence suggests that city and county land-use authorities are increasingly active in the water arena. Six out of 10 land-use departments are involved in the planning activities of at least one water utility serving their jurisdictions. Nearly as many have instituted some form of local policy to screen for water availability before approving new development. Cities and counties have responded massively to the new state "show me the water" laws, in effect since 2002, allaying some initial concerns that compliance would be lax.

Taken together, these findings suggest that California is well positioned to tackle the challenges of finding and managing water for growth. This does not mean that it will be easy or that success is inevitable. The more obvious risk of failure—and the one receiving more attention in public discussions—is on the water supply front. If growth occurs in areas with inadequate supplies, entire communities could be put at risk of chronic water shortages. But another, more hidden, risk of failure is on the housing supply front. If communities reject growth rather than finding water supply solutions compatible with it, entire generations may face the prospect of worsening housing shortages.

To avoid either scenario of failure, California's utilities and local governments face four key challenges: (1) strengthening long-term water planning, (2) streamlining water adequacy screening for new development, (3) realizing the potential of water conservation, and (4) consolidating progress in groundwater management. After examining each of these, we consider how state actions could help move things forward.

Strengthening Long-Term Water Planning

Our analysis of the 2000-round of UWMPs revealed several main weaknesses. One-sixth of eligible agencies submitted no plan whatsoever; a significant portion of submitted plans lacked detailed projections of supply and demand; and, when available, these detailed series often deviated considerably from aggregate figures presented elsewhere in the plans. A majority of utilities reported considerable normal-year surpluses, both now and 20 years hence, raising the possibility that many are banking on "paper water" for their margin of comfort.

Progress is clearly needed to bring UWMPs to the level where they can serve as a basis for assessing long-term supply reliability. The "show me the water" laws have raised the stakes, because a well-documented UWMP can be used to demonstrate water availability for new development. The next round of UWMPs, due in December 2005, should be seen as an opportunity for progress.

The record from the 2000-round drums home a consistent message: Plans are both more likely to be submitted and more likely to be complete when utilities are not working in isolation. This means involving other utilities within the region, including those providing wastewater services. (It is no coincidence that full-service utilities, which provide their own wastewater services, do far better on planning recycled water use.) It also means making the most of existing networks, including not only wholesalers but also groundwater management entities. In regions where such networks are scarce, such as the San Joaquin Valley, regional water user groups may be a particularly important alternative.

Greater regional collaboration among utilities also enables utilities to join forces and build a broader portfolio of water supply options. In this respect, members of the vast MWDSC network have a great advantage over utilities in other regions, not only because MWDSC can realize scale economies in portfolio development but also because the individual members pool the risks of local variations in supplies and demands. Utilities outside large networks are also more likely to compete among each other for new supplies.

Better water planning also means drawing in city and county land-use planners. Their involvement improves water demand planning, an area where the UWMPs are particularly weak. Up-front linkages with land-use agencies will also facilitate the coordination needed to implement some water supply solutions: recycled water use, outdoor conservation, and even some indoor conservation programs depend on such land-use decisions as zoning, building codes, and local ordinances.

Finally, plans are better when the utilities consult with the general public and local citizens' groups. An added benefit of consultation is that utilities may thereby help allay public concerns about long-term supply reliability.

The record also shows that performance was better for some types of organizational structures. As a group, municipal water departments did not do as well as special districts in complying with the requirements of the UWMP Act. On the other hand, they did better than special districts in engaging land-use authorities in the planning process. Private utilities generally did worse than either of these groups. The lesson is not that massive organizational overhaul is needed but rather that utilities and their watchdogs need to be cognizant of these weaknesses. Special districts and private utilities may benefit, for instance, by designating someone as a liaison with local land-use authorities. Of course, this is also true for some municipal departments, because coordination by this group is not universal.

Streamlining Water Adequacy Reviews

Through a combination of local and state policies, the vast majority of California's local jurisdictions now screen for long-term water availability before approving new development. This process can be justified as a way to protect communities from the risk of chronic water shortages by requiring better up-front planning. Mobilizing new supplies generally requires years of advance preparation, and in some places new supply projects can be very expensive. Without screening, developers might have incentives to build without worrying about the long-term water supply consequences.

The conundrum is how to screen without unreasonably slowing housing growth. Jurisdictions adopting screening policies since the mid-1990s have cut back significantly on issuance of residential construction permits, and it appears likely that housing growth has also been slower in cities and counties that adopted screening policies earlier. Several mechanisms are at work: longer delays before approval, downsizing or outright refusal of projects, and an increase in the climate of uncertainty surrounding the approval process.

The best way to minimize these effects while maintaining a rigorous screening process is to streamline it. This means developing sound information on long-term supply reliability and options for augmenting supplies in line with growth—in a nutshell, good long-term water planning documents. It also means finding efficient ways to pay for new supplies.

From an equity standpoint, it might be best to fund new supplies by raising water rates, a practice that would also encourage conservation. However, given likely community resistance, introducing explicit impact fees for new water may be a good alternative. Utilities set a price, based on a new home's approximate portion of new water costs. The utility, not the developer, undertakes responsibility to mobilize the new resources. Water resources become part of the buy-in fee for new development, along with other community facilities, such as schools, roads, and local water and wastewater treatment and delivery.

Such an approach, widely used in Colorado as well as Southern Nevada, should both reduce delays and remove much of the uncertainty from the approval process. A potential criticism of water resource impact fees is that they will raise the price of new housing. But if impact fees allow more housing to be built, this criticism does not necessarily hold. Paying to play may be preferable to not being invited to the game.

In this vision, streamlining reviews goes hand in hand with a policy to accommodate growth by making new water available. This is not a requirement under state law, and it is not a vision shared by all Californians. In several places, activists have tried to block new water projects to prevent development. More broadly, it is fair to wonder how many Californians view conservation as a legitimate way to make room for new growth. One telltale sign is the large number of communities that restrict new development while failing to adopt conservation policies for existing residents.

Realizing the Potential of Water Conservation

Since the early 1990s, there have been some notable successes in urban water conservation. Thanks to an aggressive low-flow toilet retrofit program, the city of Los Angeles was able to make up for supply cutbacks to mitigate environmental damage in Mono Lake and the Owens Valley. San Diego County has maintained constant levels of water use over the past decade despite population growth of more than 15 percent. More generally, CUWCC programs have encouraged utilities to adopt a range of Best Management Practices to improve water-use efficiency. But development trends point in the direction of higher water use, with more and more families locating in the hotter inland valleys, in single-family homes with high landscaping needs.

To accommodate growth, California faces a twofold conservation challenge: curbing the water demands of new housing and convincing existing residents to cut back on their water use. The picture emerging from the 2000-round of UWMPs is not encouraging on either score: The plans anticipate constant per capita use to 2020, to be met with increases in other supply sources. The trends in water pricing are not particularly encouraging, either. Progress in adopting conservation-oriented, tiered rate structures has been limited since the mid-1990s, with only half of the state's residents covered. Coverage is most limited in the fast-growing inland areas, where conservation pricing could do the most to moderate use. In the San Joaquin Valley and the Sacramento Metro region, many homes still have no meters at all.

What will it take for Californians to realize the potential of urban water conservation? Politically, it may be easier to impose conservation on new development than on existing users. Extra conservation measures and recycled water use are now conditions for approval on many large projects. Developers will go along if this is the only option. Getting existing residents to share the resource is more difficult because of the sense of entitlement that comes with existing water-rights law. As water becomes scarcer (and more expensive) statewide, there are no automatic levers to induce conservation in communities that choose not to conserve. As a case in point, residents in the Santa Clarita Valley have used the "water card" to oppose growth while facing some of the lowest (uniform) water rates in the region and using a third more water per household than the norm.[1]

Although there may be some room for such "soft" programs as public education, it is likely that incentives will be needed to make substantial progress on this front. One option is to pay existing residents to conserve. This is the principle behind using state grants or impact fees to fund programs such as retrofits and turf replacement. An alternative, but not mutually exclusive, path is to raise water fees. California water rates are still quite low in relation to median incomes. The use of tiered rate structures is a potentially powerful conservation tool, which also offers substantial equity benefits.

Consolidating Progress in Groundwater Management

Among the other potential water sources to support growth, groundwater poses the most serious management challenges at the local level. In contrast to surface water, over which the state exercises regulatory authority, groundwater is considered a local resource, whose management is the prerogative of local users. This resource is at once threatened and full of potential. Unsustainable pumping—commonly known as overdraft—is a problem in much of the San Joaquin Valley and in various other areas. It can lead to dry wells, land subsidence, and saltwater intrusion. Thanks in part to the space made available by overdraft, underground storage offers the potential to augment usable water supplies considerably.

Groundwater is the largest single source of new supplies projected by the UWMPs, and two-thirds of the increase is slated for areas outside fully managed basins. Conflicts have already begun to emerge in some of these areas, as developers plan to use groundwater to supply new housing projects. The concerns relate both to the total amount of water that can be used without causing harm and to the allocation of that water among competing users. Managed basins—run either by a water master or a special groundwater district—are able to resolve such conflicts. They

---

[1]Calculated using water fee information for the Newhall Ranch Water District and the Santa Clarita Water Company, as compared with over 80 other service areas in Los Angeles County (Black and Veatch, 2003).

99

have active monitoring systems and a well-established method for apportioning use, either through explicit water rights or through prices. In unmanaged basins, good technical information is often lacking. And without clear use-rights or pump fees, it is difficult to keep pumping to sustainable levels. Groundwater banking is also compromised when the rules are not clear.

Water users in these areas are well aware of the issues at stake, but they have been reluctant to submit to a management authority. The objections relate largely to cost: not wishing to pay pump fees for "their" water, not wishing to engage in a protracted legal battle to adjudicate use-rights. As long as groundwater is mainly used for farming, these objections may be reasonable. Numerous studies have shown that the costs of overdraft in agricultural areas are relatively low.[2] One reason is that farmers naturally reduce pumping once the water table recedes below a certain level. With urban growth, this equation changes, because municipal users can afford to pump water from much deeper wells. This is precisely why basin management has made more progress in built-up areas of Southern California than in the Central Valley.

Over the past decade, water users in many unmanaged areas have embarked on initiatives to improve basin oversight, without subjecting users to the more rigorous rules that operate in adjudicated basins or special districts. These initiatives, which take the form of groundwater management plans or joint powers authorities, have made inroads into improving the information base. In some cases, they have also made progress in managing supplies, through voluntary agreements to support basin recharge and through rules for operating groundwater banks.

As growth pressures increase, these systems will be put to the test. One question is whether voluntary cooperation models can lead to "friendly" adjudications, wherein users agree to pin themselves down to specific quantities in a nonadversarial process. A recent Southern California adjudication, among users in the fast-growing Beaumont basin, proceeded largely in this manner (Moore, 2004c). A Central Valley model might be the Sacramento Regional Groundwater Authority, which has made considerable progress in this direction. The

---

[2]For reviews of this literature, see Provencher (1995) and Knapp et al. (2003).

alternative to firmer operating rules is increasing overdraft, heightened risks of shortages for local users, and costly, protracted legal battles.

Where Can State Action Help?

Even by the standards of its western neighbors, California is very much a "home rule" state, delegating considerable authority to local entities. The local control paradigm is strong in land use but perhaps even more striking in the water arena. California is one of the few states that does not regulate groundwater use. It is also one of the few that does not directly intervene in the determination of water supply adequacy for development. In Arizona, Colorado, Nevada, and New Mexico, state engineers directly review water adequacy for projects in a significant number of cases (Hanak and Browne, 2004). Arizona delegates this responsibility only to utilities that meet strict eligibility criteria, including rigorous, regularly updated, long-term plans.

California's local entities strongly defend the home rule paradigm and demonstrate an almost reflexive opposition to state involvement in local affairs. In this political context, state policies that facilitate local action tend to be more palatable than more direct regulatory intervention.

Not surprisingly, most state policies to promote better local water and land-use planning have been facilitative in nature. The first element in the toolkit is enabling legislation. Both the Urban Water Management Plan Act and the "show me the water" laws rely on citizen enforcement rather than on direct state oversight. The same can be said for local groundwater management plans, which legislation authorized in the early 1990s. Before 2002, agencies were not even required to submit copies of the plans to DWR.

The second facilitative policy, used generously over the past several years, has been financial carrots. Thanks to the availability of billions in state water bond funds, the state has been in a position to reward local entities for taking positive actions. Legislation now makes state grants contingent on submission of a complete UWMP, gives precedence to groundwater management efforts involving multiple parties sharing the same basin, and prioritizes collaborative projects for the allocation of $500 million in integrated regional water management funds.

Given the amounts at stake, there is little doubt that such policies provide incentives. Since 2002, DWR has been able to send more than one utility back to the drawing board to include missing UWMP elements. Anecdotal evidence from the field suggests that more agencies are trying to work together than ever before. The hope is that these collaborations last beyond the duration of the state-funded bank account.

The third facilitative policy, used more sporadically than the others, is technical support. For urban water planning and water adequacy reviews, this has primarily consisted of outreach on how to comply with the law. For groundwater management, DWR has become more involved in some regions, participating in basin management initiatives and assisting in basin investigations.

Regulatory actions, meanwhile, have focused primarily on conservation. They include legislation requiring use of low-flow plumbing fixtures in new homes and, starting in 2007, the sale of water-efficient washing machines. They also include the series of laws passed over the past decade to get municipal utilities to use meters.

Significantly, the most recent meter bill, AB 2572, introduces the possibility of sanctions for noncompliance. As of 2010, not only will recalcitrant agencies be ineligible for financial assistance from the state, they may also be refused permits to augment water supplies. The State Water Resources Control Board, which oversees surface water rights, appears to be thinking along the same lines. The board recently informed the Sonoma County Water Agency that it would be reluctant to authorize increased use of Russian River water until the agency provided convincing evidence of conservation efforts (Soper, 2004).

In our view, there is more room in California's future for regulatory actions backed by sticks rather than carrots. Withholding of permits for new water rights is a potentially powerful tool to encourage local entities to manage water resources responsibly.

Financial incentives, while attractive to utilities, may not always be justified. The litmus test for public subsidies should be whether there are public benefits or equity considerations. Some of the bond funds are clearly being directed to areas of broad public benefit, such as ecosystem restoration and groundwater basin investigation and management. But many funds are going toward straightforward supply projects, including conservation. This incentive scheme may set a bad precedent if utilities (and local water users) come to expect taxpayer subsidies for projects that could be funded through water-related fees.

It may also be time to solicit a greater technical contribution from the state into the analysis of water supply reliability. Although local oversight will remain essential to the UWMP process, DWR could play a valuable role in screening plan quality. Department staff already review the plans for completeness. Going the extra steps to assess data consistency and reliability could help push utilities to improve plan content.

DWR can also perform a crucial task in helping evaluate the capacity of unmanaged groundwater basins. In most cases, developers are responsible for preparing water supply assessments. When a solid set of data on the basin is lacking, the incentives are strong for these reports to minimize potential harm to other users. DWR can serve as a neutral participant in technical basin analyses, thereby aiding the local decisionmaking process. Joint assessments involving DWR and local water agencies provide the best opportunities for pooling available data and experience on basin characteristics.

Although some of these policy shifts are not likely to be popular with local entities, they do not require a radical overhaul of the system of local control. In our view, they are more important than further refinements of local obligations under the UWMP Act or the water adequacy laws. In a few short years, the message of the water adequacy laws has gotten across. The task now facing California is to promote streamlined reviews and responsible local management of water resources.

Appendix A

California's Counties and Regions

For much of the analysis, this report puts the state's 58 counties (Figure A.1) into regional groups reflecting both economic and

Figure A.1—California's Counties

hydrologic similarities (Table A.1). The boundaries for the San
Francisco Bay Area correspond to those of the regional council of
government (COG). For Southern California, we broke with this
division to capture the different climatic and growth pressures in the
inland and coastal areas. Thus, San Diego, which has its own COG, was
grouped together with the coastal members of the Southern California
Association of Governments (SCAG). SCAG's two metropolitan inland
counties, San Bernardino and Riverside, were grouped together as the
Inland Empire. SCAG's one rural member, Imperial County, was
grouped with the rural "rest-of-the-state" counties. The Sacramento
Metro region corresponds to the four counties in the Sacramento-Yolo
Consolidated Metropolitan Statistical Area. The two other counties in
the Sacramento region's COG, Sutter and Yuba, are included in the rest-
of-the-state category. The eight counties of the San Joaquin Valley do

Table A.1

Region Definitions

Region	Counties
San Francisco Bay Area	Alameda, Contra Costa, Marin, Napa, San Francisco, San Mateo, Santa Clara, Solano, Sonoma
Central Coast	Monterey, San Benito, San Luis Obispo, Santa Barbara, Santa Cruz
Southern Coast	Los Angeles, Orange, San Diego, Ventura
Inland Empire	Riverside, San Bernardino
San Joaquin Valley	Fresno, Kern, Kings, Madera, Merced, San Joaquin, Stanislaus, Tulare
Sacramento Metro	El Dorado, Placer, Sacramento, Yolo
Rest of the state	Alpine, Amador, Butte, Calaveras, Colusa, Del Norte, Glenn, Humboldt, Imperial, Inyo, Lake, Lassen, Mariposa, Mendocino, Modoc, Mono, Nevada, Plumas, Shasta, Sierra, Siskiyou, Sutter, Tehama, Trinity, Tuolumne, Yuba

not have a regional COG, but they form a well-defined region from the standpoint of both climate and economy.

Although there is a great deal of overlap, these regions differ somewhat from the 10 hydrologic regions DWR uses in its statewide planning exercises (Figure A.2). Because many of the hydrologic boundaries do not correspond to administrative boundaries, the

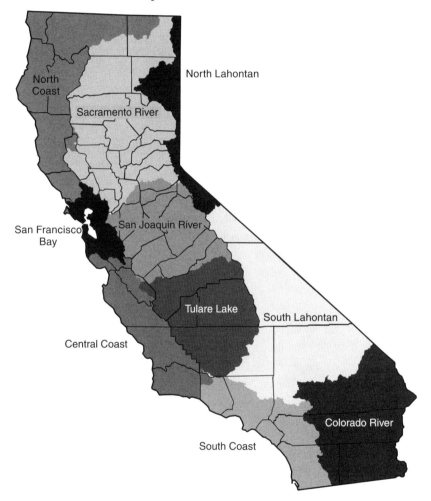

Figure A.2—Department of Water Resources Hydrologic Regions

hydrologic regions do not readily lend themselves to analysis of local government decisionmaking. For instance, San Bernardino County falls within three hydrologic regions, but information on construction permits is available only for the county as a whole.

DWR's estimates of regional patterns of water use for 2000 are presented in Table A.2. The data, derived from the annual "Water Production Survey" covering a sample of water utilities throughout the state, confirm the higher per capita levels of use in the inland areas, including the Sacramento Metro region, the San Joaquin Valley, much of the Inland Empire, and the eastern portion of Los Angeles County, which lies in the South Lahontan region. The table also shows the estimated share of outdoor water use in each region for the residential sector and overall. These detailed breakdowns appear less reliable than the aggregate use figures. For instance, the Colorado River region—a hot, mainly lowland, desert area—reports very high indoor uses and not particularly high outdoor residential uses relative to use in less harsh inland valleys. Conversely, the numbers may overstate outdoor uses and understate indoor uses in the heavily urbanized San Francisco Bay Area. For these reasons, DWR considers these estimates provisional and subject to revision.

Table A.2

Per Capita Water Use by Hydrologic Region, 2000 (in gallons per day)

	Residential			Large Landscape	Total Urban	Agriculture	Total	Population	% for Exterior Use Residential	Total Urban[a]
	Interior	Exterior	Total							
San Francisco Bay	46	51	97	13	156	16	172	6,105,650	53	41
Tulare Lake	118	124	241	9	309	5,113	5,422	1,884,675	51	43
San Joaquin River	96	117	213	17	303	3,584	3,886	1,751,010	55	44
South Coast	88	44	132	12	208	44	252	18,223,425	33	27
Colorado River	250	87	337	219	1,005	5,903	6,881	606,535	26	30
Sacramento River	77	100	177	38	296	2,998	3,294	2,593,110	57	47
Central Coast	74	42	116	6	181	621	802	1,459,205	36	27
South Lahontan	169	95	265	8	332	446	779	721,490	41	31
North Lahontan	77	55	132	22	364	4,243	4,607	99,035	41	21
North Coast	61	62	123	17	208	1,117	1,325	644,000	50	38
California	85	60	145	18	232	896	1,128	34,088,135	41	33

SOURCE: Author's calculations based on water-use and population data reported in Department of Water Resources (2005).

NOTE: DWR considers the breakdowns between indoor and outdoor uses provisional and subject to revision.

[a]Includes residential exterior and large landscapes but not outdoor uses in the commercial and industrial sector, for which there are no separate estimates.

Appendix B

Urban Water Management Plans

The Urban Water Management Plan Database

UWMP-Eligible Utilities

Before each cycle of Urban Water Management Plans, DWR prepares a list of utilities considered large enough to meet the compliance threshold (3,000 connections or 3,000 acre-feet of annual deliveries) and sends letters reminding them of the submission requirements and deadline and workshop schedules and locations. For the 2000-round, this list included 411 utilities. By July 2003, DWR had received plans from 337 utilities in this group, as well as 30 unsolicited plans.

Most of the unsolicited plans were for very small branches of one private utility, the Southern California Water Company, which submitted plans for all of its service areas. Two small retailer members of the Sonoma County Water Agency, which submitted a plan jointly with all of its members, were also among those that sent unsolicited plans. Since our interest lies in analyzing the performance of utilities required to comply with the law, we excluded 21 of these unsolicited utilities that fell well below the size threshold (fewer than 1,000 occupied households) and retained the nine utilities above that threshold, assumed to have been missed by DWR in its initial list (indeed, five of the nine had submitted plans in the 1995 UWMP round). We also removed two nonsubmitting utilities that had appeared on DWR's initial list, after determining that they were not water purveyors. This brought the total sample of eligible utilities to 418, for which 346 plans were submitted. The excluded plans account for a negligible share of state population in 2000.

Between July 2003 and August 2004, another nine eligible utilities submitted plans, as did three unsolicited utilities. The unsolicited group included two small rural Kern County agencies that are embarking on large real estate development projects; the UWMPs were drawn up to justify water supplies for these projects. The third was a plan for a new utility in Sacramento County, formed by a merger of two utilities already in our sample (both of which submitted plans). We have excluded these late submissions from the analysis owing to a lack of data on plan content. Overall, they raise the submission rate from 82 to 84 percent for eligible retail agencies and the population coverage from 77 to 78 percent.

Utility Characteristics

Designation of utility type (retailer, wholesaler, or mixed) and membership in wholesale networks was based on information from known wholesalers and was cross-checked with data reported in the UWMPs. In the eligible sample, we designate 373 utilities as retailers, 26 as wholesalers, and 19 as mixed retailers-wholesalers.[1] It was straightforward to identify utilities' organizational form—private, special district, and municipal water department—from their names. Several county-run agencies were also grouped with the municipal departments. Information on whether the utility is full-service (providing wastewater services) was obtained from the U.S. Environmental Protection Agency website, which maintains lists of all permitted wastewater agencies in the country. Information on membership in adjudicated basins or special groundwater management districts was obtained from the basin management entities.

Service Area and Community Characteristics

To get comprehensive information on service area characteristics, we developed a geographic information systems database with maps of all retail service areas, which could then be linked to the 2000 Census block group files. Service area maps were obtained from a wide range of sources, including DWR, the USBR, wholesale agencies, regional

---

[1]Retailers were defined as agencies selling less than 10 percent of their supplies to other agencies and mixed agencies as those selling 10 percent or more. The largest wholesale share for a mixed agency was 72 percent. In principle, wholesalers provide no retail services. In fact, four utilities in the wholesale group also appear to have some (relatively minor) retail functions, but we were unable to get accurate information on their retail service areas.

councils of government, and individual utilities. In about 20 cases, we hand-drew the maps based on nondigitized service area maps provided by utilities. For one eligible retailer—the Los Angeles District branch of the Cal-American Water Company—we were unable to obtain any service area map. This utility is therefore excluded from the analysis.

Only retail service areas (including those of mixed agencies) were mapped to block groups, because, by definition, wholesalers serve areas only indirectly through their retail utility clients. We treated all large landmarks (such as national, state, and county parks) as uninhabited, redistributing the population among the other areas within the block group. Although every attempt was made to produce distinct retail service areas (because retailers function as local monopolies), the different map sources led to some small areas of overlap. In such cases, the population in the overlapping area was split across both utilities.

All service area and community characteristics reported in the analysis are drawn from the 2000 Census except for one: the share of voter registration in November 2000. For this, we used the voter information database from the Institute of Government Studies at U.C. Berkeley, which is available by block group (Statewide Database, 2000).

UWMP Content

The study's plan content analysis relies on DWR's UWMP worksheets database, which tracks completeness of plan components and reports details on a number of areas, including volume data. We engaged in a substantial quality control exercise before using the data, cross-checking answers that appeared problematic in any way against the information in the plans themselves. In all, roughly 100 plans were checked directly. We were particularly strict in noting the availability of volume data, considering it to be present only when complete. For instance, in cases where a utility reported only a portion of the detailed supplies, such as the amount available from a wholesaler but not the amount of local groundwater withdrawals, we considered the detailed supply data to be missing.

For the demand management measures (DMMs), the data presented here merged results from three reporting methods. Before September 2000, utilities had to report on 16 DMMs; this was subsequently reduced to 14, to achieve compatibility with the 14 BMPs of the CUWCC. CUWCC members are eligible to submit their BMP reports in lieu of a separate demand management section within the UWMP. We use a weak measure of compliance for the DMMs, considering utilities to be in compliance if they are either implementing the measure or claiming exemption for legal, economic, or noneconomic reasons. For utilities submitting BMPs (roughly one-quarter of the sample), we took the responses from the CUWCC website and considered agencies to be in compliance if their reporting had been complete at least once since 2000. Only one BMP reporter—the city of Sacramento—had an incomplete score, with no response on metering (BMP 4). Roughly two dozen of the utilities not submitting a UWMP did submit a BMP report to the CUWCC; we have included these results in the overall compliance scores.

Measuring Planning Performance

Table B.1 provides an overview of the 57 required plan elements and the 13 volume data series, with compliance rates for our sample of 319 retailers and mixed utilities and the 26 wholesalers that submitted plans by July 2003.[2] Compliance rates tend to fall considerably when one considers whether the plans include detailed quantitative information on these elements, such as demand and supply projections.

Compliance Regressions

The regression analysis takes various measures of plan completeness as dependent variables, with a set of utility and community characteristics as explanatory factors, as described in Chapter 3. The three overall performance measures are plan submission (yes/no), an overall compliance score, and a volume data score. The overall

---

[2]Additional requirements for the 2005-round of UWMPs include required notification of cities and counties of plan preparation (AB 2552, 2000); discussion of groundwater sources and water supply projects (SB 610, 2001); discussion of quality of existing sources and effects of quality on management (AB 901, 2001); and discussion of desalination sources (SB 318, 2004).

Table B.1

Urban Water Management Plan Elements for the 2000-Round

	Retailers and Mixed Utilities		Wholesalers	
	Compliance Rate	Including Volumes	Compliance Rate	Including Volumes
I. Plan preparation	0.92		0.95	
1 Provide proof of public hearing	0.89		0.96	
2 Attach copy of adoption resolution	0.99		1.00	
3 Describe coordination of plan preparation with other agencies and the public	0.89		0.88	
II. Supply and demand planning	0.91	0.81	0.88	0.78
Service area descriptions				
1 Describe climate characteristics	0.95		0.92	
2 Provide population projections (20 years)	0.95	0.84[a]	0.92	0.85[a]
3 Describe other demographic factors	0.93		0.92	
Water supply (detailing sources)				
4 Identify water supply sources	1.00		1.00	
5 Quantify existing supply volumes	0.97	0.93	1.00	0.92
6 Quantify planned supply volumes (20 years)	0.95	0.84[a]	0.88	0.81[a]
7 Describe transfer/exchange opportunities	0.82		0.85	
Water use (detailing use by sectors)				
8 Quantify past use	0.94	0.61	0.92	0.73
9 Quantify current use	0.96	0.73	0.96	0.88
10 Quantify projected use (20 years)	0.93	0.63[a]	0.96	0.81[a]
Supply reliability				
11 Provide supply volumes for average year, single dry year, and multiple dry years	0.87	0.74	0.88	0.69
12 Describe plans to replace inconsistent sources	0.87		0.77	
13 Estimate minimum supply volumes for next three years	0.82	0.71	0.77	0.65
14 Describe reliability of supply to seasonal or climatic shortages	0.87		0.81	
15 Describe vulnerability of supply to seasonal or climatic shortages	0.85		0.77	
Supply and demand comparison				
16 Compare total supply to total projected use over next 20 years in five-year increments	0.92	0.80[b]	0.88	0.73[b]
17 Compare total supply to total projected use for different water year scenarios (normal, single dry, multiple dry)	0.82	0.69	0.81	0.69

	Retailers and Mixed Utilities		Wholesalers	
	Compliance Rate	Including Volumes	Compliance Rate	Including Volumes
III. Wastewater and recycled water	0.75	0.69	0.70	0.65
1 Describe wastewater collection and treatment systems in service area	0.91		0.85	
2 Quantify volume of wastewater collected	0.70	0.53[c]	0.69	0.54[c]
3 Quantify volume of wastewater treated	0.69	0.40[c]	0.69	0.46[c]
4 Describe methods of wastewater disposal	0.82		0.73	
5 Describe type and place of recycled water currently used	0.85		0.73	
6 Describe current recycled water use	0.87		0.81	
7 Quantify potential uses of recycled water	0.72		0.69	
8 Quantify current and projected volume of recycled water use	0.77	0.46[a]	0.73	0.58[a]
9 Describe technical and economic feasibility of serving potential recycled water uses	0.77		0.58	
10 Describe actions that could encourage recycled water use	0.70		0.69	
11 Describe projected results of taking these actions in terms of annual volume of recycled water use	0.65		0.65	
12 Provide a recycled-water-use optimization plan	0.60		0.60	
IV. Water shortage contingency plan	0.85		0.71	
1 Provide actions toward preparation of catastrophic interruption of supplies	0.91		0.85	
2 Attach copy of draft water shortage contingency resolution or ordinance	0.87		0.81	
3 Provide at least one stage of action	0.94		0.81	
4 Provide supply conditions for each stage	0.92		0.77	
5 List mandatory prohibitions against specific use practices during shortages	0.91		0.69	
6 List excessive-use penalties and discuss how applicable	0.88		0.58	
7 List consumption reduction methods supplier will use to reduce use in most restrictive stages	0.89		0.69	
8 Describe how actions and conditions affect revenues	0.77		0.69	

	Retailers and Mixed Utilities		Wholesalers	
	Compliance Including		Compliance Including	
	Rate	Volumes	Rate	Volumes
9 Describe how actions and conditions affect expenditures	0.72		0.62	
10 Describe proposed measures to overcome revenue and expenditure effects	0.71		0.62	
11 Provide mechanism(s) for determining actual reductions	0.82		0.65	
V. Demand management/BMPs	0.90		0.90	
Detailed results for DMM reports only				
1 Residential water survey programs	0.82		0.73	
2 Residential plumbing retrofit programs	0.89		0.87	
3 System water audits, leak detection, and repair	0.88		0.93	
4 Metering with commodity rates	0.92		0.87	
5 Large landscape conservation programs	0.84		0.73	
6 High-efficiency washing machine rebate programs	0.89		0.88	
7 Public information programs	0.94		0.93	
8 School education programs	0.90		0.87	
9 Commercial, industrial and institutional conservation programs	0.85		0.73	
10 Wholesale agency programs	0.99		1.00	
11 Conservation pricing	0.84		0.87	
12 Water conservation coordinator	0.77		0.87	
13 Water waste prohibitions	0.86		0.87	
14 Residential ultra-low-flow toilet replacement programs	0.89		0.80	

NOTES: Sample size for UWMP reporting is 319 retail agencies (of which 17 are mixed) and 26 wholesale agencies. For DMMs, the sample size is 230 and 15, respectively, except for DMM 6 and DMM 10, for which the count is 133 and 8.

[a]Volume data are considered complete if available in 2020.

[b]Volume data are considered complete if available at five-year intervals to 2020.

[c]Volume data are considered complete if available in 2000.

compliance score takes a weighted average of all 57 plan elements, with weighting used to highlight the relative importance of each section. The following weights are used: general preparation—5 percent (unchanged); supply and demand planning—40 percent (versus 30% unweighted); wastewater and recycling—15 percent (versus 21% unweighted); drought contingency planning—20 percent (versus 19% unweighted); demand management measures—20 percent (versus 25% unweighted). Regressions were also run for completeness of these individual plan components. All measures of completeness are scaled from zero to one.

For determinants of UWMP submission, the most appropriate regression method is a binomial probit model. For completeness scores, the preferred method is a two-tailed Tobit, which allows for the bunching of responses at both zero and one. Here we report results for the entire sample of 391 retail and mixed agencies.[3] Table B.2 summarizes the regression results for the three main compliance variables. For explanatory variables that can take many values, such as size or home prices, it shows the effects on plan performance of a one standard deviation increase over the sample mean. For categorical variables, such as whether the utility is full-service, it shows the effects of belonging to that group. In the case of UWMP submission, these effects refer to the probability of submitting a plan. For the other two measures, they show the percentage increase in plan completeness attributable to each variable. Summary descriptive statistics for the dependent and independent variables overall and by region are presented in Tables B.3 and B.4, respectively. Detailed regression results for the overall compliance measures and for individual plan components are presented in Table B.5.

---

[3]Separate runs using only the retail agencies did not generate substantively different results. Two controls for wholesale activity—a dummy variable for the mixed agencies and a variable measuring the share of wholesale sales in the total—were insignificantly different from zero, making it possible to reject the hypothesis that the mixed agencies have different compliance behavior.

Table B.2

Determinants of UWMP Performance

	UWMP Submission	Overall Compliance	Volume Data
Utility characteristics			
Wholesaler plan quality	0.16***	0.29***	0.19***
Full-service utility	0.05	0.16**	0.10*
Size (91,000 homes above mean)	0.20	0.02	0.03
Organizational form (base case: special district)			
Municipal department	−0.07	−0.18***	−0.12**
Private utility	−0.19***	−0.20***	−0.37***
Community characteristics			
Median home price ($152,000 above mean)	−0.04**	−0.07*	−0.07
Homeowner rate (13% above mean)	−0.02	−0.04	−0.03
Voter registration rate (13% above mean)	0.06***	0.10***	0.10***
Growth pressures			
Share of new homes (12% above mean)	−0.03	−0.05	−0.04
Number of new homes (65,000 above mean)	−0.22	0.01	0.00
Share*number of new homes	0.21	0.02	0.03
Region (base case: San Joaquin Valley)			
Southern California[a]	0.12**	0.36***	0.18**

NOTES: For complete regression results, see Table B.5. For variables with values listed in parentheses, the table reports the effect on performance of a one standard deviation increase above the sample mean. Otherwise, it reports the effect of moving from a value of zero to one.

*Indicates that the coefficient is different from zero at the 90 percent confidence level in a two-tailed test.

**Indicates that the coefficient is different from zero at the 95 percent confidence level in a two-tailed test.

***Indicates that the coefficient is different from zero at the 99 percent confidence level in a two-tailed test.

[a]The table reports the estimated increase in performance rates as compared with the San Joaquin Valley. For most performance measures, statistical tests show that Southern California's performance rates are also significantly higher than those of other regions except the Central Coast.

Table B.3
Summary Statistics for UWMP Compliance Scores

	California	Censored observations Zero	One	Bay Area	San Joaquin Valley	Southern Coast	Inland Empire	Sacramento Metro	Central Coast	Rest of the State
Submitted UWMP	0.82			0.77	0.64	0.93	0.84	0.92	0.75	0.59
	(0.39)			(0.43)	(0.49)	(0.26)	(0.37)	(0.27)	(0.44)	(0.50)
Overall compliance score	0.72	53	110	0.66	0.51	0.87	0.78	0.72	0.66	0.44
	(0.35)			(0.34)	(0.41)	(0.25)	(0.36)	(0.27)	(0.40)	(0.38)
Volume data score	0.56	79	42	0.50	0.44	0.65	0.61	0.56	0.55	0.36
	(0.35)			(0.36)	(0.41)	(0.29)	(0.34)	(0.31)	(0.38)	(0.36)
Supply and demand score	0.74	73	200	0.63	0.49	0.90	0.81	0.76	0.67	0.50
	(0.39)			(0.39)	(0.43)	(0.27)	(0.37)	(0.3)	(0.44)	(0.45)
Supply and demand volume data	0.61	79	108	0.54	0.45	0.72	0.67	0.63	0.60	0.39
	(0.37)			(0.38)	(0.42)	(0.31)	(0.36)	(0.33)	(0.42)	(0.38)
Drought contingency planning	0.69	80	190	0.64	0.48	0.84	0.75	0.72	0.61	0.37
	(0.4)			(0.42)	(0.45)	(0.31)	(0.39)	(0.28)	(0.45)	(0.40)
Wastewater and recycling score	0.56	86	65	0.49	0.42	0.69	0.67	0.45	0.51	0.28
	(0.38)			(0.37)	(0.41)	(0.32)	(0.36)	(0.35)	(0.43)	(0.38)
Demand management	0.79	57	263	0.85	0.59	0.89	0.79	0.81	0.76	0.47
	(0.37)			(0.33)	(0.47)	(0.26)	(0.37)	(0.36)	(0.41)	(0.44)
Sample size	391			60	44	148	51	26	28	34

NOTES: The table reports sample means with standard deviations in parentheses. The wastewater and recycling score is a strict measure, excluding components if volume data are missing.

Table B.4

Summary Statistics for Utility and Community Characteristics

	California	Bay Area	San Joaquin Valley	Southern Coast	Inland Empire	Sacramento Metro	Central Coast	Rest of the State
Utility characteristics								
Wholesaler plan quality	0.47	0.56	0.10	0.77	0.33	0.30	0.13	0.15
	(0.43)	(0.31)	(0.25)	(0.33)	(0.47)	(0.34)	(0.29)	(0.29)
Full-service utility	0.40	0.42	0.77	0.25	0.45	0.31	0.46	0.47
	(0.49)	(0.50)	(0.42)	(0.43)	(0.50)	(0.47)	(0.51)	(0.51)
Size (100,000s of homes served)	0.27	0.50	0.16	0.34	0.17	0.21	0.11	0.09
	(0.91)	(1.46)	(0.27)	(1.11)	(0.2)	(0.3)	(0.1)	(0.14)
Municipal water department	0.50	0.58	0.73	0.47	0.43	0.35	0.43	0.47
	(0.50)	(0.50)	(0.45)	(0.50)	(0.50)	(0.49)	(0.50)	(0.51)
Private utility	0.18	0.13	0.16	0.24	0.08	0.15	0.21	0.15
	(0.38)	(0.34)	(0.37)	(0.43)	(0.27)	(0.37)	(0.42)	(0.36)
Community characteristics								
Median home price ($100,000s)	2.34	3.86	1.14	2.65	1.32	1.78	2.98	1.25
	(1.52)	(1.94)	(0.63)	(1.27)	(0.48)	(0.65)	(1.57)	(0.41)
Share of homeowners	0.62	0.64	0.60	0.61	0.66	0.63	0.60	0.61
	(0.13)	(0.11)	(0.08)	(0.15)	(0.11)	(0.14)	(0.12)	(0.15)
Share of eligible adults registered to vote	0.68	0.69	0.60	0.70	0.63	0.72	0.76	0.69
	(0.13)	(0.10)	(0.14)	(0.14)	(0.11)	(0.09)	(0.14)	(0.12)

Table B.4 (continued)

	California	Bay Area	San Joaquin Valley	Southern Coast	Inland Empire	Sacramento Metro	Central Coast	Rest of the State
Growth pressures								
Share of homes built 1990–2000	0.15	0.14	0.20	0.10	0.21	0.21	0.14	0.17
	(0.12)	(0.11)	(0.11)	(0.09)	(0.14)	(0.18)	(0.09)	(0.09)
Number of homes built 1990–2000 (10,000s)	0.32	0.37	0.29	0.34	0.34	0.40	0.13	0.20
	(0.65)	(0.59)	(0.46)	(0.87)	(0.43)	(0.48)	(0.09)	(0.45)
Share*number of homes built 1990–2000	0.06							
	(0.14)							
Sample size	391	60	44	148	51	26	28	34
	100%	15%	11%	38%	13%	7%	7%	9%

Table B.5

UWMP Compliance Regressions

	Submitted UWMP	Overall Compliance	Volume Data Score	Supply and Demand Planning	Supply and Demand Volume Data	Drought Contingency Planning	Wastewater and Recycling Planning	Demand Management Planning
Utility characteristics								
Wholesaler plan quality	0.16***	0.29***	0.19***	0.63***	0.30***	0.39**	0.24***	0.85***
	(0.05)	(0.07)	(0.06)	(0.16)	(0.09)	(0.16)	(0.08)	(0.26)
Full–service utility	0.05	0.16**	0.10*	0.27**	0.02	0.34**	0.30***	0.24
	(0.04)	(0.07)	(0.06)	(0.14)	(0.08)	(0.15)	(0.07)	(0.22)
Size (100,000s of homes served)	0.22	0.02	0.03	0.06	0.05	0.03	0.02	0.46
	(0.20)	(0.06)	(0.05)	(0.10)	(0.07)	(0.11)	(0.06)	(0.92)
Municipal water department[a]	-0.07	-0.18***	-0.12**	-0.36**	-0.13	-0.24	-0.16**	-0.88***
	(0.05)	(0.07)	(0.06)	(0.14)	(0.08)	(0.15)	(0.07)	(0.24)
Private utility[a]	-0.19***	-0.20***	-0.37***	-0.63***	-0.53***	-0.48***	-0.29***	-0.02
	(0.08)	(0.08)	(0.07)	(0.17)	(0.10)	(0.17)	(0.08)	(0.28)
Community characteristics								
Median home price ($100,000s)	-0.03**	-0.05*	-0.05**	-0.08*	-0.06**	-0.09	-0.03	-0.11
	(0.02)	(0.02)	(0.02)	(0.05)	(0.03)	(0.05)	(0.03)	(0.08)

Table B.5 (continued)

	Submitted UWMP	Overall Compliance	Volume Data Score	Supply and Demand Planning	Supply and Demand Volume Data	Drought Contingency Planning	Wastewater and Recycling Planning	Demand Management Planning
Share of homeowners	-0.13	-0.32	-0.25	-0.54	-0.19	-0.03	-0.38	-0.65
	(0.17)	(0.27)	(0.23)	(0.56)	(0.33)	(0.59)	(0.27)	(0.88)
Share of eligible adults registered to vote	0.44***	0.75***	0.71***	1.08**	0.94***	1.34**	0.66**	2.40**
	(0.17)	(0.27)	(0.24)	(0.54)	(0.33)	(0.58)	(0.27)	(0.88)
Growth pressures								
Share of homes built 1990–2000	-0.28	-0.43	-0.38	-0.60	-0.68*	-1.34*	-0.03	-1.65
	(0.24)	(0.33)	(0.29)	(0.67)	(0.41)	(0.70)	(0.34)	(1.11)
Number of homes built 1990–2000 (10,000s)	-0.34	0.07	0.03	0.01	0.00	0.07	0.07	0.34
	(0.28)	(0.12)	(0.10)	(0.25)	(0.14)	(0.25)	(0.13)	(0.92)
Share*number of homes built 1990–2000	1.50	0.14	0.18	0.57	0.29	0.03	0.24	0.12
	(0.96)	(0.41)	(0.35)	(0.90)	(0.50)	(0.83)	(0.44)	(2.07)
Region[b]								
Southern California	0.12**	0.36***	0.18**	0.88***	0.25**	0.85***	0.35***	0.26
	(0.06)	(0.10)	(0.09)	(0.20)	(0.12)	(0.22)	(0.10)	(0.32)
Central Coast	0.04	0.20	0.12	0.47*	0.17	0.33	0.17	0.12
	(0.06)	(0.13)	(0.12)	(0.25)	(0.16)	(0.28)	(0.14)	(0.41)

Table B.5 (continued)

	Submitted UWMP	Overall Compliance	Volume Data Score	Supply and Demand Planning	Supply and Demand Volume Data	Drought Contingency Planning	Wastewater and Recycling Planning	Demand Management Planning
Bay Area	0.04	0.10	0.05	0.05	0.01	0.24	0.10	0.58
	(0.06)	(0.12)	(0.11)	(0.23)	(0.15)	(0.25)	(0.12)	(0.40)
Sacramento Metro	0.10	0.14	0.10	0.34	0.12	0.39	0.04	0.09
	(0.04)	(0.13)	(0.12)	(0.25)	(0.16)	(0.27)	(0.13)	(0.43)
Rest of the state	−0.09	−0.20*	−0.18	−0.21	−0.25*	−0.42*	−0.24*	−0.96**
	(0.09)	(0.12)	(0.11)	(0.23)	(0.15)	(0.25)	(0.13)	(0.37)
Log-likelihood	−151.81	−290.19	−274.03	−320.33	−340.49	−350.39	−306.66	−285.21
Probability of the chi-square	0.00	0.00	0.00	0.00	0.00	0.00	0.00	0.00

NOTE: All regressions include a constant, not reported here.

*Indicates that the coefficient is different from zero at the 90 percent confidence level in a two-tailed test.

**Indicates that the coefficient is different from zero at the 95 percent confidence level in a two-tailed test.

***Indicates that the coefficient is different from zero at the 99 percent confidence level in a two-tailed test.

[a]The base case for organizational form is special districts.

[b]The base case for regional effects is the San Joaquin Valley.

The following provides some additional information on variable definitions and alternative specifications used:

Wholesale plan quality. This variable is set to the value of "volume data" for the UWMP of the retailer's direct wholesale provider. That is, if an agency is a member of the MWDSC network, but actually contracts with one of MWDSC's secondary wholesalers, such as the San Diego County Water Authority or the Inland Empire Utilities Agency, this variable takes the value of volume data for the secondary wholesaler. Regressions were also run with a simple wholesale network membership dummy variable. Although membership is positive and significant when included on its own, it loses its significance when included together with the wholesale plan quality variable. This suggests that wholesale planning quality is a more important factor than membership alone. Regressions were also run including a dummy variable to measure membership in a managed groundwater basin. This variable is not significant—not surprising in light of the fact that basin management agencies do not submit UWMPs, and hence (we assume) play no coordinating role in plan submission by their members.

Size. The only way to get a uniform measure of utility size was by using census data, because water delivery data from the utilities themselves are incomplete. Our preferred measure of size is the number of households, a direct measure of residential connections. Although this measure implicitly assumes that commercial and industrial uses are proportionate to residential use, which is not strictly true, there is no systematic way to adjust for these other uses. For the mixed agencies and a handful of retailers with small amounts of water sales to other agencies (generally smaller local utilities), we augmented this size variable by the proportion of water sales to local deliveries. In separate regressions, we also attempted to capture the fact that both density and the proportion of multifamily to total houses affect the total amount of water delivered, by reducing outdoor landscaping needs. When size was weighted by density—either units per acre or the share of single-family homes in the housing stock—it remained insignificant.

Housing values. For utilities with more than one block group, we took the average of the median home values for all block groups, weighted by the share of homes in each block group. Runs were also done using income instead of home value, with similar results.

Political participation. To calculate the share of the eligible population registered to vote, we took the number of registered voters as a share of the estimated number of adult citizens. This last variable was calculated by multiplying the adult population for the block group by the share of citizens in that block group. This implicitly assumes that noncitizens are distributed evenly across minor and adult age groups. We use voter registration, rather than voter turnout, because the latter has fluctuated considerably in recent elections as a function of the items on the ballot. This variable was also subjected to some specification tests. Voter registration is known to be correlated with race, with a higher proportion of whites registered than other groups. When the share of whites in the population is included in the regressions, it has a higher standard error than voter registration, suggesting that registration is correctly capturing the political participation measure, not just acting as a proxy for race. We also ran some regressions with a measure of ideology—the share of Republicans among registered voters. This variable is always negative but insignificant. Other tests used an alternative measure of political participation—the presence of local growth controls. Two measures were used, drawing on city surveys conducted in the late 1980s and late 1990s (see Appendix C for a detailed description of these variables). Although these measures both were of positive sign, neither was significant, and when included together with the measure of voter registration, the latter variable remained significant.

Growth pressures. We used two measures of growth pressures: the number and share of homes built between 1990 and 2000, as well as an interaction term, which should be significant if there are effects in particularly high growth areas, experiencing both large absolute increases and a high proportion of new housing in the total housing stock.

Region. We used the seven regional breakdowns presented elsewhere in the study, with one exception: The Southern Coast and the Inland Empire were combined, because they consistently had very close coefficient estimates and significance levels. The six counties in this group all have utilities belonging to the MWDSC network, and some other utilities also cut across county boundaries. We tested for whether the superior performance of Southern California utilities was attributable to the MWDSC network but found this not to be the case—an MWDSC dummy is insignificant, and the Southern California regional dummy remains significant when it is included.

Public Outreach and the Planning Process

Chapter 3 also reports some results regarding the role of utility outreach to other agencies and the public in plan performance. DWR's worksheets provide detailed information on the extent to which utilities engage in this process, drawing on the descriptions provided in the plans. Specifically, they record which other agencies and public groups were notified about plan preparation and were engaged in the process itself (helped write or commented on drafts or attended public meetings). To provide a simple summary measure, we tallied the number of times a utility engaged in this outreach activity, drawing the distinction between contacts with other agencies (wholesalers, retailers, wastewater agencies, and local governments) and with the general public and citizens' groups.

We then ran the same set of regressions on overall plan performance as above, this time including the participation measures as a potential explanatory factor. Because we have this measure only for the 319 utilities that submitted plans, these regressions are run only for that subset of eligible utilities. Table B.6 reports the descriptive statistics and the regression results. Although the outreach variables are significant, the effects are not very large: A 15 percent increase in public outreach leads to a 3 percent improvement in overall compliance and volume data scores.

Table B.7 reports the results of regressions that show which factors are associated with public and agency outreach, drawing on a subset of the utility and community characteristics used above. As noted in Chapter 3, political participation is, as might be expected, associated with higher rates of public outreach, and special districts outperform other utilities in this regard. For agency outreach, utility characteristics

Table B.6
Role of Public and Agency Outreach in UWMP Performance

	Mean (Std. Dev.)	Dependent Variable			
		Overall Compliance Score	Overall Compliance Score	Volume Data Score	Volume Data Score
Outreach activities					
Other agencies	0.12 (0.14)	0.28*** (0.09)		0.40*** (0.11)	
Public outreach	0.09 (0.15)		0.22*** (0.08)		0.23** (0.10)
Utility characteristics					
Wholesaler plan quality	0.52 (0.42)	0.04 (0.03)	0.05 (0.03)	0.03 (0.04)	0.05 (0.04)
Full-service utility	0.40 (0.49)	0.11*** (0.03)	0.11*** (0.03)	0.06* (0.04)	0.06* (0.04)
Size (100,000s of homes served)	0.30 (1.00)	0.01 (0.02)	0.01 (0.02)	0.01 (0.03)	0.01 (0.03)
Municipal water department[a]	0.50 (0.5)	-0.06** (0.03)	-0.07** (0.03)	-0.04 (0.04)	-0.05 (0.04)
Private utility[a]	0.15 (0.36)	-0.08** (0.04)	-0.08** (0.04)	-0.18*** (0.05)	-0.20*** (0.05)
Community characteristics					
Median home price ($100,000s)	2.36 (1.43)	-0.01 (0.01)	-0.01 (0.01)	-0.01 (0.01)	-0.01 (0.02)

Table B.6 (continued)

	Mean (Std. Dev.)	Dependent Variable			
		Overall Compliance Score	Overall Compliance Score	Volume Data Score	Volume Data Score
Share of homeowners	0.62	0.07	0.09	-0.03	0.00
	(0.13)	(0.13)	(0.13)	(0.15)	(0.16)
Share of eligible adults registered to vote	0.69	0.04	0.03	0.12	0.11
	(0.13)	(0.13)	(0.13)	(0.16)	(0.16)
Growth pressures					
Share of homes built 1990–2000	0.15	-0.32**	-0.30**	-0.31*	-0.28
	(0.12)	(0.15)	(0.15)	(0.19)	(0.19)
Number of homes built 1990–2000 (10,000s)	0.34	0.02	0.02	0.03	0.03
	(0.70)	(0.05)	(0.05)	(0.06)	(0.06)
Share*number of homes built 1990–2000	0.07	0.03	0.03	0.03	0.02
	(0.15)	(0.17)	(0.17)	(0.21)	(0.21)
Region[b]					
Southern California	0.56	0.20***	0.20***	0.01	0.01
	(0.5)	(0.05)	(0.05)	(0.06)	(0.06)
Central Coast	0.07	0.15**	0.16**	0.03	0.04
	(0.25)	(0.06)	(0.06)	(0.08)	(0.08)
Bay Area	0.14	0.00	0.01	-0.11	-0.09
	(0.35)	(0.06)	(0.06)	(0.07)	(0.07)
Sacramento Metro	0.08	0.02	0.01	-0.07	-0.09
	(0.26)	(0.06)	(0.06)	(0.08)	(0.08)

Table B.6 (continued)

	Mean (Std. Dev.)	Dependent Variable			
		Overall Compliance Score	Overall Compliance Score	Volume Data Score	Volume Data Score
Rest of the state	0.06	-0.10	-0.09	-0.10	-0.10
	(0.24)	(0.06)	(0.06)	(0.08)	(0.08)
Censored values (dependent variable = 1)		110	110	42	42
Sample mean		0.87	0.87	0.69	0.69
		(0.17)	(0.17)	(0.25)	(0.25)
Sample size	319	319	319	319	319
Log-likelihood		-31.43	-32.45	-56.64	-60.20
Probability of the chi-squared		0.00	0.00	0.00	0.00

NOTES: One-tailed Tobit models. All regressions include a constant, not reported here

*Indicates that the coefficient is different from zero at the 90 percent confidence level in a two-tailed test.

**Indicates that the coefficient is different from zero at the 95 percent confidence level in a two-tailed test.

***Indicates that the coefficient is different from zero at the 99 percent confidence level in a two-tailed test.

aThe base case for organizational form is special districts.

bThe base case for regional effects is the San Joaquin Valley.

Table B.7

Factors Associated with Utility Outreach

	Dependent Variable		
	Mean (Std. Dev.)	Agency Outreach	Public Outreach
Utility characteristics			
Wholesale network membership	0.70	0.05**	–0.01
	(0.46)	(0.02)	(0.04)
Full-service utility	0.40	0.03	0.06**
	(0.49)	(0.02)	(0.03)
Size (100,000s of homes served)	0.30	0.00	–0.02
	(1.00)	(0.01)	(0.02)
Municipal water department[a]	0.50	–0.05**	–0.08**
	(0.5)	(0.02)	(0.03)
Private utility[a]	0.15	–0.13***	–0.08*
	(0.36)	(0.03)	(0.04)
Community characteristics			
Median home price ($100,000s)	2.36	–0.01	–0.02
	(1.43)	(0.01)	(0.01)
Share of homeowners	0.62	0.03	–0.31**
	(0.13)	(0.09)	(0.13)
Share of eligible adults registered to vote	0.69	0.11	0.35**
	(0.13)	(0.10)	(0.15)
Region[b]			
Southern California	0.56	–0.02	0.02
	(0.5)	(0.04)	(0.06)
Central Coast	0.07	0.03	0.03
	(0.25)	(0.05)	(0.08)
Bay Area	0.14	0.07	0.14**
	(0.35)	(0.05)	(0.07)
Sacramento Metro	0.08	–0.11**	0.01
	(0.26)	(0.05)	(0.07)
Rest of the state	0.06	–0.03	–0.03
	(0.24)	(0.05)	(0.07)
Sample size	319	319	319
Censored values (dependent variable = 0)		80	140
Sample mean		0.12	0.09
		(0.14)	(0.15)

	Mean	Agency Outreach	Public Outreach
Log-likelihood		32.01	–83.70
Probability of the chi-square		0.00	0.11

NOTES: One-tailed Tobit regressions. All regressions include a constant, not reported here.

*Indicates that the coefficient is different from zero at the 90 percent confidence level in a two-tailed test.

**Indicates that the coefficient is different from zero at the 95 percent confidence level in a two-tailed test.

***Indicates that the coefficient is different from zero at the 99 percent confidence level in a two-tailed test.

aThe base case for organizational form is special districts.

bThe base case for regional effects is the San Joaquin Valley.

are important: Not surprisingly, agencies in wholesale networks are more likely to make these contacts.[4]

Projecting Supply and Demand

Because not all utilities provided data on supply sources and demand levels, it was necessary to extrapolate to draw a picture of the aggregate. For this purpose, we let missing utilities take the values of reporting utilities within their region. For 2000, we derived regional averages by taking the sum of volumes reported and the sum of population within the service areas of reporting utilities from the 2000 Census block group information.[5] We then augmented the totals by the share of regional population not included in the sample. For 2020 values, we used the official population projections available at the time the UWMPs were done (summarized in Department of Finance, 2001). DOF's May 2004 release reduced the projections of future growth, a factor that the 2005-

---

[4]These regressions include membership in a wholesale network rather than wholesale plan quality, as membership had a lower standard error.

[5]It was necessary to rely on an external source of population data, rather than the population figures provided by the UWMPs themselves, because these series were incomplete and in some cases inaccurate.

round of UWMPs will likely take into account. Table B.8 reports the detailed results for 2000 and 2020 supplies by region and shows the share of each region for which data were reported.

This extrapolation method is most susceptible to error in regions where a large portion of the population is not covered by reporting utilities. The problem is greatest in counties in the rest of the state, where, in addition, there is no reason to believe that water-use patterns are homogeneous (per capita use is much higher in the desert climate of Imperial County, for instance, than in humid, temperate Humboldt County). For this reason, we do not count the values from this region in the statewide totals. The other region with a low rate of UWMP coverage is the San Joaquin Valley. For future supply sources, it is likely that the extrapolation overstates the share of wholesaler supplies expected in this region, because reporting utilities rely on wholesalers more than those not reporting data. Correspondingly, it is likely that our method understates increased groundwater use in the San Joaquin Valley

Table B.8

Water Supply Sources for Retail Service Areas, 2000 and 2020 (thousands of acre-feet)

	Bay Area		Central Coast		Southern Coast		Inland Empire		San Joaquin Valley		Sacramento Metro		California[a]	
	2000	2020	2000	2020	2000	2020	2000	2020	2000	2020	2000	2020	2000	2020
Water sources														
Federal water projects	254	266	42	44	13	19	0	1	35	35	169	169	537	561
State Water Project	117	126	57	57	24	24	56	56	0	0	0	0	265	276
Wholesalers	427	545	2	2	2,037	2,377	167	252	352	691	94	145	3,219	4,207
Own groundwater	87	92	267	307	958	1,242	625	922	993	1,388	365	471	3,446	4,637
Own surface water	631	654	46	49	487	493	17	22	0	0	320	484	1,570	1,786
Transfers and exchanges	5	5	0	0	9	21	16	22	0	10	15	73	47	138
Recycling	14	58	3	15	97	349	36	112	4	14	3	18	165	595
Other[b]	117	183	55	60	347	454	191	351	55	263	20	43	820	1,420
Total	1,652	1,930	473	533	3,973	4,977	1,109	1,738	1,439	2,403	986	1,404	10,069	13,619
Population (thousands)	6,852	8,338	1,395	1,992	16,205	19,997	2,768	5,619	3,303	5,144	1,728	2,604	33,712	45,822
Share in reporting utilities	61%		40%		78%		69%		29%		80%		64%	

SOURCES: Population: 2000 (Census); 2020 (Department of Finance, 2001). Utility data are from 248 agencies with retail service areas that reported detailed supply sources in both 2000 and 2020.

[a]Statewide figures assign the average for all other regions to counties in the rest of the state.

[b]"Other" is a grab-bag category including desalination, new wholesale sources, new storage, and new exchanges.

Appendix C

Housing Supply Effects of Water Adequacy Screening

The theoretical literature on housing markets predicts that growth controls of various types will slow housing growth and raise housing prices.[1] The primary focus of the empirical literature in this field has been on measurement of the price effects of regulation, impact fees in particular.[2] These studies, which rely on micro-level data on home and lot sales to estimate hedonic equations, generally confirm the theoretical prediction of higher price effects. The key debates have been on the different effect of fees on existing and new housing and undeveloped lots.

An alternative approach, developed most fully by Mayer and Somerville (2000a), is to measure the effects of growth controls on the supply of housing. In their framework, new housing is a function of current and lagged changes in home prices, changes in real interest rates, and growth control measures. The model specification—treating changes in housing supply as a function of changes in prices, rather than price levels—represents a departure from many previous studies of housing supply and yields estimates of the impact of regressors on the steady-state level of housing growth.[3]

Mayer and Somerville apply this model to estimate the effects of general growth controls and impact fees on new single-family residential construction in 44 metropolitan statistical areas (MSAs) between 1985

---

[1]For models considering quantity-type growth controls, see Helsley and Strange (1995) and Brueckner (1999). For models focusing on the effects of impact fees, see Brueckner (1997) and Yinger (1998).

[2]See Singell and Lillydahl (1990), Skaburskis and Qadeer (1992), Dresch and Sheffrin (1997), and Ihlanfeldt and Shaughnessy (2004).

[3]For a presentation of the theoretical underpinnings of the model, see Mayer and Somerville (2000b). For an earlier study of housing supply effects of impact fees, see Skidmore and Peddle (1998).

and 1996. The study uses quarterly data on construction permits and prices, and single-point-in-time measures of growth controls from a Wharton School survey conducted at the midpoint of the time period under analysis. Measures of regulation include the estimated number of months to subdivision approval, a count of the number of growth management techniques introduced in the MSA, and a dummy variable indicating the presence of impact fees in cities in the MSA. They find that both nonprice measures of growth controls significantly reduce the steady-state level of residential construction but that the presence of impact fees is insignificant. In particular, a one-month increase in the delay to approval of subdivisions decreases supply by 10 to 12 percent, and each additional growth management technique decreases supply by 7 percent.

Model and Data

The Mayer and Somerville framework is appropriate to the analysis of housing supply effects of local water adequacy regulations in California. The model specified here considers annual jurisdiction-specific new home construction as a function of changes in housing prices and interest rates and a set of growth management tools, including water adequacy screening policies, water impact fees, and measures of general growth controls at two points in time.

Our data have several advantages over the Mayer and Somerville study. First, because we have jurisdiction-specific data on both policies and number of construction permits issued, we are able to match the incidence of growth management policies directly with the local land-use authority, thus avoiding aggregation biases. Second, the availability of time-series data on two key measures—water adequacy screening policies and water impact fees—allows for the fixed-effects estimation of impacts of policy changes over time. This controls for the possible omission of other local characteristics that might affect residential construction, such as physical barriers (mountains, bodies of water, or national parks) and history.

The results presented here show fixed- and random-effects regressions for balanced panels from the mid-1990s to 2003.[4] The mid-1990s starting point is chosen for two reasons. First, 1994 marked the end of a multiyear decline in residential construction. Between 1988 and 1993, the number of annual permits fell from over 250,000 units to only a third that level. Analysis going back to 1990, the first year for which data are available on residential permits, generates less consistent results concerning the effects of regulation.[5] It is likely that the slack nature of the housing market in the early 1990s made growth controls less binding. Second, some data sources, notably for water connection fees, are not consistently available before the mid-1990s. The main regressions start in 1994; those including water connection fees start in 1995.

The following is a brief description of data sources and characteristics of the variables used and their expected effects on housing supply.

Residential Home Construction

New home construction, the dependent variable, is measured by the number of residential construction permits issued, obtained from the Construction Industry Research Board. In the roughly 4 percent of cases where zero permits were issued in a year, this value is reset to one to allow the variable to be specified in natural logs.[6]

---

[4]The random-effects estimator assumes a common error component for each cross-sectional unit that is orthogonal to the regressors. The coefficients reflect the effects of variation both between cross-sectional units and within these units over time. The fixed-effects estimator sweeps out the effects of all cross-sectional variation; its coefficients reflect the effects of within-unit variation.

[5]In the city-only samples, the water adequacy screening policies continue to register significant negative effects with regressions starting in the early 1990s, but this is not the case with the full sample before 1994.

[6]Various alternative specifications, including a model run in levels, a model increasing all permit values by one, and a model dropping zero-valued observations, confirm that this adjustment does not substantially alter the results for the variables of interest.

Housing Prices

The results presented here use the quality-constant housing price index from the Office of Federal Housing Enterprise Oversight (OFHEO) for the metropolitan statistical area in which the local jurisdiction is located. As such, it represents a measure of home price movement within the general real estate market of the area.[7] Series are available for 25 MSAs, covering from one to three counties.[8] Prices enter the regression as the growth between first-quarter previous year and first-quarter current year, plus one lag. This specification reduces the likelihood of any simultaneity bias. Because first-quarter home prices reflect contracts negotiated six to 12 weeks before closing, our measure of home prices is a lagging measure of price. Meanwhile, the number of construction permits is a leading measure of supply; most of the new homes will not be put on the market until the following year, and some may not ever be built. Both price variables are expected to be positively associated with new housing growth, because price increases send a signal to builders of excess demand. The coefficients measure short-term price elasticities.

Real Prime Interest Rate

Arithmetic changes in the real prime interest rate are a measure of the cost of capital to builders and are expected to be negatively associated with housing growth. The model does not incorporate another potential

---

[7]The OFHEO data are not without limitations. In periods of high refinancing activity, such as 2002–2003, they have been found to underreport price increases, because some refinancing occurs without full reappraisals. Also, the series excludes homes with values in excess of the limits for underwriting by federal mortgage programs (in 2004, $333,700). For coastal California MSAs, where many homes exceed this value, the index captures price movements in only a subset of the distribution. An alternative measure of housing prices used was the median home sales price by jurisdiction, obtained from the California Association of Realtors. Although this series captures local market effects, it is less complete, precluding estimation of a representative balanced panel before 1997. A comparison of results using the MSA price data and the local price data generates identical results for the key variables of interest, and similar price elasticity effects, suggesting that the use of the MSA price variable is justified.

[8]Jurisdictions in 18 rural counties included in the regressions were assigned the values of the nearest MSA. If multiple options were available, this choice was based on the location of the nearest shopping hub. Regressions excluding the jurisdictions from these counties yield very similar results to those presented here.

measure of builder costs—the index of construction costs—which exhibits very little cross-regional variation in California.

Water Adequacy Rule

A variable measuring the presence of a local water adequacy screening policy, derived from our survey of land-use planners, takes the value of one in years when a jurisdiction has a policy in place and zero otherwise. The results presented here include those jurisdictions for which a policy start date was missing (just under a third of those with policies), with the start date set to the survey sample mean, 1988. Because recent start dates are more likely to be known by survey respondents, jurisdictions with missing adoption years probably have had screening policies in place for some time, if not as far back as 1988. Because our analysis does not start until the mid-1990s, inclusion of these jurisdictions does not influence the estimates of the effects of policy adoption in the fixed-effects regressions; they are differenced out. They do contribute to the estimates in the random-effects regressions. Their inclusion substantially lowers the standard error of parameter estimates on the water adequacy rule variable, suggesting that the use of the full sample is appropriate. Because water adequacy screening is a form of growth management, we expect the coefficient to be negative.

The model does not attempt to measure the effect of the state water adequacy laws. There is reason to believe that the 1995 law has not had effects distinct from local policies, because no outreach was done following its passage and local awareness of the requirements appears to have been very low. Although the new laws, effective since January 2002, are definitely generating review activity, it is unlikely that they had significant effects on the number of permits issued during 2002 or 2003. Reviews under SB 610 (at the environmental review stage) typically occur several years before the start of construction, and even reviews under SB 221 (before final subdivision mapping) take place well before the issuance of building permits. It is probable that all projects receiving permits in 2002 had already gone through the subdivision process and were thereby exempt from either law.

Water Connection Fees

Data on water-related impact fees for new homes were obtained from biannual, odd-year surveys of water utilities conducted by an engineering consulting firm (Black and Veatch, various years). The survey records typical new home connection fees by utility and by local jurisdiction. In cases where more than one utility provides services in an area, the variable takes a simple average of fees charged. The results presented here interpolate the off-survey-year values as the average of the prior and subsequent year.[9] These data enter the regressions in two ways: as a binary variable indicating whether an impact fee was charged (comparable to the specification in many other growth control models, including Mayer and Somerville), and as growth rates between preceding and current-year levels (comparable to the measure of home prices).[10] To allow for this log specification, impact fees of zero were set to one dollar. An alternative specification, with fee changes in levels, is also presented.

Because in California these fees are generally levied to contribute to the costs of local infrastructure rather than to the cost of acquiring new water supplies, the use of impact fees is a distinct growth management tool. Because both the presence and an increase in the magnitude of the impact fees could raise costs of construction, they might be expected to be negatively associated with the growth in housing. However, to the extent that such fees constitute a payment for services, rather than a tax, it is also possible that they will not affect housing growth. In this case, the fee is readily recouped by builders through a corresponding increase in home prices and does not distort household demand (Dresch and Sheffrin, 1997; Ihlanfeldt and Shaughnessy, 2004). The income effects of fee increases may nevertheless lead to a downward pressure on housing demand.

In our sample period, water impact fees moved from an average of $1,419 to $2,183 per home.[11] Over a quarter of all communities do not

---

[9]This specification provides a better fit than taking either the lead or lag values for the off-survey year. Using the maximum fee charged within an area, rather than the average, yields higher standard errors.

[10]We also ran specifications including lagged values of fee changes, to allow for adjustment over more than one period, but the coefficient was insignificant.

[11]This represents a relatively small proportion of total impact fees, which can include components for wastewater, education, transportation, and other local services.

levy fees. Fees changed in just under a third of all observations, with roughly 20 percent declining and the remainder increasing. Fees were introduced or dropped in roughly 10 percent of all cases. As with prices, the coefficients on fee changes measure short-term elasticities.

General Growth Controls

Two city surveys are used to provide single-point-in-time indicators of general growth control measures. Glickfeld and Levine's growth control measures, obtained in a statewide survey of cities in 1988, have been used in several other studies (e.g., Brueckner, 1998; Levine, 1999). We use their measure of the total number of residential, commercial, and other growth control regulations within a city.[12] In 1998 and 1999, Lewis and Neiman (2000) conducted a survey of growth management measures in cities within three major regions—Southern California, the San Francisco Bay Area, and the Central Valley—a sample excluding the Central and Northern coastal areas and low-population inland rural counties. We use a measure of the total number of residential growth control regulations recorded.[13] Because these are both time-invariant

The model thus implicitly assumes that changes in other fees are proportional to changes in water fees across jurisdictions.

[12]The maximum count is 15, including (1) adoption of a growth management element in the general plan, (2) formal population caps, (3) annual limits on residential building permits, (4) formal links between residential growth and adequate levels of public services, (5) reduction in residential density through plan amendments or rezoning, (6) requirement of voter approval to increase residential density, (7) requirement of supermajority council vote to increase residential densities, (8) redesignation of residential land to agriculture or open space, (9) annual or other limit on square footage for commercial development, (10) annual or other limits on square footage for industrial development, (11) requirement of adequate service levels before commercial or industrial development, (12) redesignation of land previously designated for commercial or industrial development, (13) adoption of height restrictions for commercial or office buildings within the last five years, (14) adoption of an urban limit line, and (15) adoption of other growth control or growth management measures. See Glickfeld and Levine (1992).

[13]The maximum count is nine, including (1) recent significant reductions in land zoned for residential use, (2) annual limits on building permits, (3) annual caps on residential units, (4) annual caps on multifamily units, (5) formal population caps, (6) links between residential growth and external formulas, such as the county growth rate, (7) use of design review standards, (8) use of public works projects to control growth, and (9) formal links between residential growth and attainment of traffic standards. The measure excludes use of caps on annual water connections, which 4 percent of

measures, they do not influence the fixed-effects estimators used here. However, they do allow us to establish whether the water adequacy policies are distinct from general growth control measures in the random-effects models.

Pre-1990 Housing Stock

An additional jurisdiction-specific control introduced in the random-effects regressions is the size of the pre-existing housing stock, drawn from the 2000 Census SF3 sample files. This variable enters the model in log form.

Data Samples

Because the various data sources on growth control measures draw from overlapping, but not identical, samples, inclusion of all measures simultaneously would severely curtail the number of observations. To preserve as many observations as possible, we have therefore opted to present the results for five samples, representing slightly different experiments. Table C.1 presents the descriptive statistics for each sample.

The "Full Sample" includes all jurisdictions responding to our land-use survey for which data on residential permits are available over the entire time period, including 31 counties and 263 cities. "Cities I" contains only the 263 cities, to allow for the possibility that the effects of water adequacy screening policies are less systematic in unincorporated areas. "Cities II" is the subset of 224 cities that are also included in Glickfeld and Levine's 1988 growth management survey. "Cities III" is the subset of 163 cities for which data are available from Lewis and Neiman's survey. The "Water Fee" sample includes data from the 193 jurisdictions (185 cities and eight counties) for which time-series data on water connection fees were available. The jurisdictions in the Water Fee

---

respondents reported (a comparable figure to our survey). Tests were also done using two other measures: the aggregate of up to four ballot-box measures available to limit growth and the respondent's judgment as to whether growth was a highly controversial issue in the city. None of the three measures were associated with the presence of a water adequacy policy. In contrast to the measure presented here, the latter two were not significantly associated with housing growth either.

Table C.1

Housing Supply Regressions, Descriptive Statistics, 1994–2003

	Full Sample	Cities I	Cities II	Cities III	Water Fee Sample, 1995–2003
Residential construction permits issued	259	234	256	271	359
(units per year)	(674)	(610)	(654)	(612)	(844)
Change in real prime rate	−0.12				−0.30
	(1.12)				(1.03)
MSA price growth rate	0.05				0.06
	(0.07)				(0.07)
Pre-1990 housing stock (units)	22,278	20,803	23,036	19,539	29,543
	(80,395)	(82,940)	(89,810)	(39,548)	(98,219)
Water adequacy rule	0.52	0.49	0.49	0.46	0.53
	(0.50)	(0.50)	(0.49)	(0.50)	(0.50)
Growth controls, 1988			2.09		
			(2.07)		
Growth controls, 1998–1999				1.81	
				(1.29)	
Water connection fee (binary)					0.71
					(0.45)
Water fee growth rate					0.09
					(0.71)
Water fee level change ($)					97
					(509)
Number of observations	2,940	2,630	2,230	1,680	1,737
Number of jurisdictions	294	263	223	168	193
New water adequacy policies in period t	27	26	24	13	17
Add/drop connection fees in period t					20

NOTES: The table reports sample means with standard deviations in parentheses. For interest rates and home prices, these values are virtually unchanged across samples covering the same time period.

sample are somewhat larger (as measured by the size of the pre-1990 housing stock) and have experienced more residential growth since the mid-1990s.

Results

Table C.2 presents the results of the fixed-effects regressions for the basic model with and without unincorporated areas (Full Sample and

Table C.2

Housing Supply and Water Adequacy, Fixed-Effects Models, 1994–2003
Dependent variable: Ln (residential permits)

	Full Sample	Cities I	Cities II	Cities III
Change in real prime rate	0.01	0.04	−0.01	−0.01
	(0.02)	(0.03)	(0.03)	(0.03)
MSA price growth rate	2.11***	2.05***	2.20***	1.98***
	(0.42)	(0.46)	(4.9)	(0.60)
MSA price growth rate (t − 1)	1.18***	1.20***	1.06**	1.43***
	(0.36)	(0.39)	(0.41)	(0.51)
Water adequacy rule	−0.25*	−0.26*	−0.30**	−0.52**
	(0.13)	(0.14)	(0.15)	(0.21)
Semi-elasticity of water adequacy rule	*−0.22*	*−0.23*	*−0.26*	*−0.41*
Number of observations	2,940	2,630	2,230	1,680
Number of groups	294	263	223	168
R-squared (within)	0.05	0.05	0.05	0.05

NOTES: Standard errors are in parentheses. All models contain a constant, not reported here. The semi-elasticity of water adequacy reports the exponential transformation of the parameter estimate on this binary variable.

*Indicates that the coefficient is different from zero at the 90 percent confidence level in a two-tailed test.

**Indicates that the coefficient is different from zero at the 95 percent confidence level in a two-tailed test.

***Indicates that the coefficient is different from zero at the 99 percent confidence level in a two-tailed test.

Cities I) and the samples for which other growth control data are available (Cities II and III). These regressions measure the effects of water adequacy rules for the roughly 10 percent of the sample that adopted policies after 1994. This variable is significant in all samples and of the expected sign. The longitudinal elasticities imply that jurisdictions adopting a water adequacy screening procedure reduced new housing by 22 percent (Full Sample) to as much as 41 percent in the subset of cities in Southern California, the San Francisco Bay Area, and the Central Valley (Cities III).

To see whether these housing supply effects are also present for jurisdictions that adopted water adequacy screening policies before the period under analysis, we next examine the results of random-effects regressions, which jointly measure the effects of longitudinal and cross-sectional variation in the sample (Table C.3). Hausman specification tests fail to reject the null hypothesis of no fixed effects at conventional significance levels, suggesting the absence of omitted cross-sectional variables that would bias the random-effects results.

For the Full Sample and Cities I, water adequacy rules have the expected negative sign but the coefficients attain only marginal levels of significance (p = 0.15 and p = 0.12, respectively). However, for Cities II and Cities III, this parameter is significant at the 95 percent level of confidence. Across the four samples, the implied reduction in annual housing growth for jurisdictions that undertake screening before approving residential development ranges from 13 to 25 percent, somewhat lower than the estimates from the fixed-effects regressions. Given the results of the Hausman tests, we can consider the random- and fixed-effects parameters as providing the likely range of responses to regulation.

The results also confirm that water adequacy rules are not simply acting as a proxies for other growth controls. The exclusion of the growth control measures changes neither the parameter estimates nor the standard errors on water adequacy rules reported here for the Cities II and III samples (results available upon request). In contrast to water adequacy rules, both general growth control measures are positively associated with new housing. This may reflect the endogenous nature of

Table C.3

Housing Supply, Water Adequacy, and Growth Controls, Random-Effects Models, 1994–2003
Dependent variable: Ln (residential permits)

	Full Sample	Cities I	Cities II	Cities III
Change in real prime rate	0.01	0.00	–0.00	–0.01
	(0.02)	(0.03)	(0.03)	(0.03)
MSA price growth rate	2.07***	2.01***	2.17***	1.90***
	(0.42)	(0.46)	(0.49)	(0.61)
MSA price growth rate (t – 1)	1.17***	1.19***	1.07***	1.38***
	(0.35)	(0.39)	(0.41)	(0.51)
Ln (pre-1990 housing stock)	0.93***	0.89***	0.89***	0.85***
	(0.06)	(0.06)	(0.07)	(0.09)
Water adequacy rule	–0.14	–0.16	–0.27**	–0.29**
	(0.10)	(0.11)	(0.11)	(0.15)
Semi-elasticity of water adequacy rule	*–0.13*	*–0.15*	*–0.23*	*–0.25*
Growth controls, 1988			0.07*	
			(0.04)	
Growth controls, 1998–1999				0.17**
				(0.08)
Number of observations	2,940	2,630	2,230	1,680
Number of groups	294	263	223	168
R-squared (overall)	0.40	0.35	0.38	0.29
Hausman test result	0.89	0.97	0.87	0.82

NOTES: Standard errors are in parentheses. All models contain a constant, not reported here. The semi-elasticity of water adequacy reports the exponential transformation of the parameter estimate on this binary variable. For the Hausman test, the table reports the probability that the difference in coefficients between the random- and fixed-effects regressions is not systematic. For the Cities II sample, the Hausman test result reported is for regressions beginning in 1995, as the model failed to meet the required asymptotic assumptions for runs beginning in 1994.

*Indicates that the coefficient is different from zero at the 90 percent confidence level in a two-tailed test.

**Indicates that the coefficient is different from zero at the 95 percent confidence level in a two-tailed test.

***Indicates that the coefficient is different from zero at the 99 percent confidence level in a two-tailed test.

growth controls: Communities facing the most growth pressure may be more likely to adopt such measures. The relevant experiment of growth control effects would be whether adoption slows the subsequent pace of growth.[14]

The significant, negative impact of water adequacy screening rules is unlikely to be an artifact of endogeneity bias. In particular, if stronger growth were leading to the adoption of the rules, this would bias the coefficient toward zero, not away from it.[15]

Table C.4 presents the results of fixed-effects models for the Water Fee sample, adding water connection fees to the basic model.[16] In Model 1, the fee changes are expressed in percentage terms; in Model 2, they enter as changes in dollar amounts. Both models include a dummy variable to capture the presence or absence of fees. Water adequacy rules remain negatively associated with housing growth, with effects within the ranges noted above.

The story is somewhat different for impact fees. Although the adoption of fees (captured by the binary measure) does have a negative coefficient, it is not significant at conventional levels in either model, precluding a conclusion that that the adoption of fees negatively influences growth in subsequent periods. Fee changes are insignificant, whether measured in percentage or in level terms.

In sum, we estimate that between 1994 and 2003, local screening policies—present in over half of all jurisdictions—may have reduced housing growth by as much as 7 to 12 percent statewide and by an even

---

[14]In some simple regressions comparing housing levels in 1980 and 1990, Levine (1999) finds no overall effects of the presence of the growth control measures from the Glickfeld and Levine survey. In recent work using the same growth control data, Quigley and Raphael (2004) find that supply elasticities may be lower for cities with higher-than-average growth controls.

[15]We also tested whether local policy adoption is related to higher growth in previous periods by conducting granger causality tests, regressing water adequacy policies on up to four lags of the policies themselves and residential permits. Past permitting behavior had no effect on policy adoption, suggesting the absence of a systematic bias in the adoption of local screening as a response to growth.

[16]We do not present the results of random-effects models, which Hausman tests show to be biased. In these regressions, the presence of impact fees is significantly positively associated with growth, reflecting the prevalence of these fees as a financing mechanism in fast-growing communities.

Table C.4

Housing Supply, Water Adequacy, and Water Fees, Fixed-Effects Models, 1995–2003

Dependent variable: Ln (residential permits)

	Model 1	Model 2
Change in real prime rate	–0.02	–0.02
	(0.03)	(0.03)
MSA price growth rate	1.97***	1.97***
	(0.53)	(0.53)
MSA price growth rate (t – 1)	0.89*	0.90**
	(0.45)	(0.45)
Water adequacy rule	–0.42**	–0.42**
	(0.18)	(0.18)
Semi-elasticity of water adequacy rule	*–0.34*	*–0.34*
Water connection fee (binary)	–0.21	–0.23
	(0.18)	(0.17)
Semi-elasticity of water connection fee	*–0.19*	*–0.20*
Water fee level change ($)		0.00
		(0.05)
Water fee growth rate	–0.01	
	(0.04)	
R-squared (within)	0.04	0.04

NOTES: Number of observations: 1,737; number of groups: 193. Standard errors are in parentheses. All models contain a constant, not reported here. The semi-elasticities of water adequacy and water connection fees report the exponential transformation of the parameter estimates on these binary variables.

*Indicates that the coefficient is different from zero at the 90 percent confidence level in a two-tailed test.

**Indicates that the coefficient is different from zero at the 95 percent confidence level in a two-tailed test.

***Indicates that the coefficient is different from zero at the 99 percent confidence level in a two-tailed test.

larger margin in some subsets of cities.[17] This effect would be diminished, however, if developers shifted some activity to jurisdictions without screening policies. Meanwhile, water impact fees are not a drag on growth.

In all samples and specifications, other variables included in the regressions are of the expected signs, although the coefficient on the prime rate is statistically insignificant. The combined market house price elasticities for t and t − 1 are in the range of 3.2 to 3.4 percent in the runs using the full sample and the cities samples and slightly lower (2.9%) in the water fees sample runs, which begin a year later. This range is substantially lower than the short-term elasticities over five quarters found by Mayer and Somerville (15%), who used the same data source for prices but for a national sample over a different time period. It may be that the use of annual values diminishes the estimated short-term price responsiveness or that the California market since the mid-1990s exhibits less responsiveness to signals of excess demand than the national market did in the preceding decade.[18]

Finally, although there is a strong positive association between the magnitude of housing growth in this period and the size of the pre-1990 housing stock, the range of elasticities (0.85 to 0.93) indicates that smaller jurisdictions may be growing slightly faster.

---

[17]These estimates are based on the results of the random- and fixed-effects estimations for the Full Sample, using the formula: (exp(beta*sample mean) − 1).

[18]For instance, in a national study using over 80 MSAs, Saks (2004) finds that housing supply price elasticities are significantly lower in MSAs with higher-than-average growth controls (including California MSAs). As a test of whether local jurisdictions with water adequacy rules had lower price elasticities, we ran regressions interacting the rule and the price elasticities. These terms were insignificant.

Appendix D

Adoption of Increasing Block Rate Water Pricing

Table D.1 presents the results of several linear probability regressions for increasing block rate adoption, controlling for utility type and including an interaction term for jurisdictions with both local water adequacy screening policies and a municipal water department. The models include a variable for private utilities; the omitted utility type is special-purpose public water agencies. They also include population served, a control for utility size, because larger utilities may have a technical advantage in switching to these more sophisticated rates.[1]

Models 2 and 3 control for average summer temperature (April to October).[2] The water conservation advantages of increasing block rate structures are greatest in hotter climates, where landscaping uses increase considerably. Model 3 includes a measure of years since adoption of the water adequacy screening policy, to allow for the possibility that it may take some time to change the rate structure. The regressions treat each utility/local government pair as a unit of observation, meaning that some local governments appear more than once in the sample, as do some utilities.[3]

In 2003, 44 percent of California utilities for which we have a complete set of data used increasing block rates, and another 1 percent

---

[1]For an empirical model of increasing block rate adoption using national data, see Hewitt (2000). Mullin (2003) updates this analysis and provides a political-economic framework for assessing the links between the utility's institutional form and adoption of increasing block rates.

[2]Annual precipitation was also included in some runs; it was not significant and did not alter the results presented here.

[3]The tables report unweighted regressions, which are appropriate insofar as some utilities vary rate structures across different jurisdictions within their service areas. Regressions weighting for the number of times a utility appears in the sample generate very similar results.

Table D.1

Adoption of Increasing Block and Peak Rate Pricing
Dependent variable: increasing block or peak rate

	Descriptive Statistics	Model 1	Model 2	Model 3
Water adequacy rule	0.62	0.01	0.01	0.05
	(0.49)	(0.07)	(0.07)	(0.09)
Years with water rule	10.27			0.00
	(11.35)			(0.00)
Water rule and city utility	0.21	0.03	0.02	0.02
	(0.40)	(0.11)	(0.11)	(0.11)
City water utility	0.37	−0.16*	−0.15*	−0.15*
	(0.48)	(0.09)	(0.09)	(0.09)
Private water utility	0.19	−0.46***	−0.43***	−0.43***
	(0.39)	(0.07)	(0.07)	(0.07)
Average summer temperature	67.58		−0.02***	−0.02***
	(5.20)		(0.01)	(0.01)
Service-area population (100,000s)	1.80	0.02***	0.02***	0.02***
	(3.83)	(0.01)	(0.01)	(0.01)
Constant		0.53***	1.62***	1.62***
		(0.07)	(0.36)	(0.36)
Increasing block or peak rate	0.45			
	(0.50)			
Adjusted R-squared		0.12	0.14	0.14
Number of observations	302	302	302	302

NOTES: Descriptive statistics report sample mean and standard deviation in parentheses. Models 1–3 report results of linear probability regressions, with standard errors in parentheses.

*Indicates that the coefficient is different from zero at the 90 percent confidence level in a two-tailed test.

**Indicates that the coefficient is different from zero at the 95 percent confidence level in a two-tailed test.

***Indicates that the coefficient is different from zero at the 99 percent confidence level in a two-tailed test.

used uniform rates with peak summer prices. Because peak rates are also considered a form of conservation pricing, we include these utilities in our sample of adopters.

The analysis confirms the absence of a relationship between the presence of a local water adequacy screening policy and the use of conservation pricing. Moreover, there is no evidence that the subset of jurisdictions with their own water departments are more likely to adopt this rate structure: The coefficient on the interaction term is positive but not statistically significant. Nor does our (admittedly crude) measure of adjustment enhance adoption of increasing block rates. As discussed in Chapter 5, factors that do make a difference are size, utility type, and summer temperature.

References

Alanez, Tonya, "Two Groups Sue to Stop Water Shipments; One Attorney Contends the Transfers Are a Way for Developers to Claim That Adequate Supplies Exist for Future Santa Clarita Valley Projects," *Los Angeles Times*, March 28, 2005.

Ashton, William J., and M. B. Bayer, "Water Supply and Urban Growth Planning: A Partnership," American Water Resources Association, *Water Resources Bulletin*, Vol. 1, No. 5, October 1983, pp. 779–783.

Association of California Water Agencies, *Water Supply and Development: A User's Guide to California Statutes Including SB 221 (Kuehl) and SB 610 (Costa)*, prepared by McCormick, Kidman, and Behrens, Sacramento, California, 2002.

Baumann, Duane D., John J. Boland, and W. Michael Hanemann, *Urban Water Demand Management and Planning*, McGraw-Hill, New York, 1997.

Benjamin, Marc, "Shaver Lake Faces Water Shortage. Residents Not Allowed to Tap Water from Lake," *Fresno Bee*, September 28, 2004.

Black and Veatch, *California Water Charge Survey*, Management Consulting Division, Irvine, California, 1991, 1993, 1995, 1997, 1999, 2001, 2003.

Brueckner, Jan K., "Infrastructure Financing and Urban Development: The Economics of Impact Fees," *Journal of Public Economics*, Vol. 66, 1997, pp. 383–407.

Brueckner, Jan K., "Testing for Strategic Interaction Among Local Governments: The Case of Growth Controls," *Journal of Urban Economics*, Vol. 44, 1998, pp. 438–467.

Brueckner, Jan K., "Modeling Urban Growth Controls," in Arind Panagariya, Paul R. Portney, and Robert M. Schwab (eds.), *Environmental and Public Economics: Essays in Honor of Wallace E. Oates*, Elgar, Cheltenham, United Kingdom, 1999.

California Urban Water Agencies, *California Urban Water Agencies Urban Water Conservation Potential,* Sacramento, California, August 2001.

California Urban Water Agencies, *Urban Water Conservation Potential: 2003 Technical Update*, Sacramento, California, July 2004.

CALFED, *Economic Evaluation of Water Management Alternatives*, Sacramento, California, October 1999.

CALFED, *CALFED Bay-Delta Program Finance Plan*, Sacramento, California, December 2004.

Cavanagh, Sheila M., W. Michael Hanemann, and Robert N. Stavins, "Muffled Price Signals: Household Water Demand under Increasing-Block Prices," Fondazione Eni Enrico Mattei Working Paper No. 40.2002, Venice, Italy, June 2002.

Chesnutt, Thomas W., and Janice A. Beecher, "Conservation Rates in the Real World," *Journal of the American Water Works Association*, Vol. 90, No. 2, February 1998, pp. 60–70.

Dalhuisen, Jasper M., Raymond J.G.M. Florax, Henri L.F. de Groot, and Peter Nijkamp, "Price and Income Elasticities of Residential Water Demand: A Meta-Analysis," *Land Economics*, Vol. 79, No. 2, May 2003, pp. 292–308.

Department of Finance, data series corresponding to *Population Projections by Race/Ethnicity, Gender and Age for California and Its Counties 2000–2050*, Sacramento, California, May 2004.

Department of Finance, *Interim County Population Projections*, Sacramento, California, June 2001.

Department of Water Resources, *Urban Water Use in California*, Sacramento, California, 1994.

Department of Water Resources, *1995 Urban Water Management Plan Review*, Sacramento, California, 1998.

Department of Water Resources, *Water Recycling 2030: Recommendations of California's Recycled Water Task Force*, Sacramento, California, June 2003a.

Department of Water Resources, *Water Desalination: Findings and Recommendations*, Sacramento, California, October 2003b.

Department of Water Resources, *Guidebook for Implementation of Senate Bill 610 and Senate Bill 221 of 2001*, Sacramento, California, October 2003c.

Department of Water Resources, *California's Groundwater*, Bulletin 118-Update 2003, Sacramento, California, October 2003d.

Department of Water Resources, California Water Plan Update*,* Bulletin 160-05, Public Review Draft, Sacramento, California, April 2005.

Dresch, Marla, and Steven M. Sheffrin, *Who Pays for Development Fees and Exactions?* Public Policy Institute of California, San Francisco, California, 1997.

Fausset, Richard, "Environmentalists File Lawsuit to Block 'Water Banking' Plan. Critics Say Program, Which Would Store Supplies for Times of Drought, Will Spur More Development in Santa Clarita Valley," *Los Angeles Times*, November 8, 2002.

Fausset, Richard, "Newhall Project Gets OK to Build," *Los Angeles Times,* November 28, 2003.

Foster, Kathryn A., *The Political Economy of Special Purpose Government*, Georgetown University Press, Washington, D.C., 1997.

Fresno Bee, "Our Views in Brief: Water Meters Save Water," September 6, 2004.

Gleick, Peter H., Dana Haasz, Christine Henges-Jeck, Veena Srinivasan, Gary Wolf, Katherine Kao Cushing, and Amardip Mann, *Waste Not, Want Not: The Potential for Urban Water Conservation in California*, Pacific Institute for Studies in Development, Environment, and Security, Oakland, California, November 2003.

Glennon, Robert J., "'Because That's Where the Water Is': Retiring Current Water Uses to Achieve the Safe-Yield Objective of the Arizona Groundwater Management Act," *Arizona Law Review*, Vol. 33, 1991, pp. 89–114.

Glickfeld, Madelyn, and Ned Levine, *Regional Growth . . . Local Reaction: The Enactment and Effects of Local Growth Control and Management Measures in California,* Lincoln Institute of Land Policy, Cambridge, Massachusetts, 1992.

Governor's Office of Planning and Research, *General Plan Guidelines*, Sacramento, California, 2003.

Groves, David, Scott Matyac, and Tom Hawkins, "Quantified Scenarios of 2030 California Water Demand," in Department of Water Resources, California Water Plan Update, Bulletin 160-05, Public Review Draft, Vol. IV, Sacramento, California, April 2005.

Hanak, Ellen, *Who Should Be Allowed to Sell Water in California? Third Party Issues and the Water Market*, Public Policy Institute of California, San Francisco, California, 2003.

Hanak, Ellen, and Margaret K. Browne, *Linking Housing Growth to Water Supply: The American West's New Frontier*, Working Paper 2004.08, Public Policy Institute of California, San Francisco, California, June 2004.

Hanak, Ellen, and Antonina Simeti, *Water Supply and Growth: A Survey of California City and County Land-Use Planners*, Occasional Paper, Public Policy Institute of California, San Francisco, California, March 2004.

Hanak, Ellen, and Ada Chen, "Going Off the Grid: Unintended Consequences of Western Water Policy," paper presented at the Western Economics Association Annual Meetings, San Francisco, California, July 4–7, 2005.

Hanemann, W. Michael, and Julie A. Hewitt, "A Discrete/Continuous Choice Approach to Residential Water Demand under Block Rate Pricing," *Land Economics,* Vol. 71, 1995, pp. 173–192.

Hayhoe, Katharine, et al., "Emissions Pathways, Climate Change, and Impacts on California," *Proceedings of the National Academy of Sciences,* Vol. 101, No. 34, August 2004, pp. 12422–12427.

Hecht, Peter, "Skeptics Challenge Water Meters," *Sacramento Bee,* December 2, 2001.

Helsley, Robert W., and William C. Strange, "Strategic Growth Controls," *Regional Science and Urban Economics*, Vol. 25, 1995, pp. 435–460.

Hewitt, Julie A., "An Investigation into the Reasons Why Water Utilities Choose Particular Residential Rate Structures," in Ariel Dinar (ed.), *The Political Economy of Water Pricing Reforms*, Oxford University Press for the World Bank, New York, 2000.

Hundley, Norris, *The Great Thirst: Californians and Water, A History,* University of California Press, Berkeley, California, revised edition, 2001.

Ihlanfeldt, Keith R., and Timothy M. Shaughnessy, "An Empirical Investigation of the Effects of Impact Fees on Housing and Land Markets," *Regional Science and Urban Economics*, Vol. 34, No. 6, 2004.

Johnson, Hans, "California's Population in 2025," in Ellen Hanak and Mark Baldassare (eds.), *California 2025: Taking on the Future*, Public Policy Institute of California, San Francisco, California, July 2005.

Johnson, Karen E., and Jeff Loux, *Water and Land Use: Planning Wisely for California's Future*, Solano Press Books, Point Arena, California, 2004.

Knapp, Keith, Marca Weinberg, Richard Howitt, and Judith Posnikoff, "Water Transfers, Agriculture, and Groundwater Management: A Dynamic Economic Analysis," *Journal of Environmental Management* Vol. 67, No. 4, 2003, pp. 291–301.

Legislative Analyst's Office, *Proposition 50 Resources Bond: Funding Eligibility of Private Water Companies*, Sacramento, California, May 2004.

Levine, Ned, "The Effects of Local Growth Controls on Regional Housing Production and Population Redistribution in California," *Urban Studies*, Vol. 36, No. 12, 1999, pp. 2047–2068.

Lewis, Paul, and Max Neiman, *Residential Development and Growth Control Policies: Survey Results from Cities in Three California Regions*, Public Policy Institute of California, San Francisco, California, July 2000.

Lewis, Paul G., and Max Neiman, *Cities Under Pressure: Local Growth Controls and Residential Development Policy*, Public Policy Institute of California, San Francisco, California, 2002.

Little Hoover Commission, *Special Districts: Relics of the Past or Resources for the Future?* Sacramento, California, May 2000.

Lucero, Lora, "Water and the Disconnects in Growth Management," *The Urban Lawyer*, Vol. 34, No. 4, 1999, pp. 871–881.

Lund, Jay, Richard E. Howitt, Marion W. Jenkins, Tingju Zhu, Stacy K. Tanaka, Manuel Pulido, Melanie Tauber, Randall Ritzema, and Inês Ferriera, *Climate Warming and California's Water Future*, Report 03-1, Center for Environmental and Water Resource Engineering, University of California, Davis, March 2003.

Mayer, Christopher J., and C. Tsuriel Somerville, "Land Use Regulation and New Construction," *Regional Science and Urban Economics*, Vol. 30, 2000a, pp. 639–662.

Mayer, Christopher J., and C. Tsuriel Somerville, "Residential Construction: Using the Urban Growth Model to Estimate Housing Supply," *Journal of Urban Economics*, Vol. 48, 2000b, pp. 85–109.

Mayer, Peter W., William B. DeOreo, Eva M. Opitz, Jack C. Kiefer, William Y. Davis, Benedykt Dziegielewski, and John Olaf Nelson, *Residential End Uses of Water*, AWWA Research Foundation and American Water Works Association, Denver, Colorado, 1999.

Mercer, Lloyd, and W. Douglas Morgan, "An Estimate of Residential Growth Controls' Impact on House Prices," in M. Bruce Johnson (ed.), *Resolving the Housing Crisis*, Ballinger Publishing Company, Cambridge, Massachusetts, 1982, pp. 189–215.

Metropolitan Water District of Southern California, *The Regional Urban Water Management Plan for the Metropolitan Water District of Southern California*, Los Angeles, California, December 2000.

Michelsen, Ari A., J. Thomas McGuckin, and Donna M. Stumpf, *Effectiveness of Residential Water Conservation Price and Nonprice Programs*, AWWA Research Foundation and American Water Works Association, Denver, Colorado, 1999.

Moore, Steve, "Cherry Valley Group Sues Development: It Challenges Beaumont's Purchase of State Water for a Housing Project," *Riverside Press-Enterprise,* January 9, 2004a.

Moore, Steve, "Water Crucial to Project. A Disagreement Exists on Whether There Is Enough for Noble Creek Vistas to Be Developed," *Riverside Press-Enterprise*, November 5, 2004b.

Moore, Steve, "Agreement Clarifies Water Usage Rights in Beaumont Basin: A Panel Drawn from Five Agencies Will Oversee Pumping. Key Users Are Factored In," *Riverside Press-Enterprise*, December 11, 2004c.

Mullin, Megan, "Specialization and Responsiveness in Local Policymaking: The Case of Water Districts," paper presented at the 2003 Meetings of the American Political Science Association, Philadelphia, Pennsylvania, August 28–31, 2003.

National Research Council, *Privatization of Water Services in the United States: An Assessment of Issues and Experience*, National Academy Press, Washington, D.C., 2002.

Neumark, David, "California's Economic Future and Infrastructure Challenges," in Ellen Hanak and Mark Baldassare (eds.), *California 2025: Taking on the Future*, Public Policy Institute of California, San Francisco, California, July 2005.

Ostrom, Vincent, Robert Bish, and Elinor Ostrom, *Local Government in the United States*, Institute for Contemporary Studies Press, San Francisco, California, 1988.

Page, G. William, "Planning Implications of Water Supply Decisions," *Planning Practice and Research*, Vol. 16, Nos. 3–4, 2001, pp. 281–292.

Planning and Management Consultants, Ltd., *Analysis of Residential Landscape Irrigation in Southern California*, prepared for the Metropolitan Water District of Southern California, Los Angeles, California, December 1991.

Provencher, Bill, "Issues in the Conjunctive Use of Surface Water and Groundwater," in Daniel Bromley (ed.), *Handbook of Environmental Economics*, Blackwell Publishers, Cambridge, Massachusetts, 1995.

Quigley, John M., and Stephen Raphael, "Regulation and the High Cost of Housing in California," mimeo, University of California, Berkeley, October, 2004.

Ricardi, Nicholas, and Richard Fausset, "Newhall Says It Has Enough Water: The Developer Is Criticized for Relying on a Private Company for Some of the Supply," *Los Angeles Times*, December 3, 2002.

Sakrison, Rodney, "New Urbanism, Growth Management and the Effect on Metropolitan Water Demands," in *Responsible Water Stewardship*, Proceedings of the Conserv 96 Responsible Water Management Conference, Orlando, Florida, January 4–8, 1996, American Water Works Associations, Denver, Colorado, 1995.

Saks, Raven, "Job Creation and Housing Construction: Constraints on Employment Growth in Metropolitan Areas," mimeo, Harvard University, Boston, Massachusetts, 2004.

Sanders, W., and C. Thurow, "Role of Land Use Planning in Water Conservation," *Proceedings of the National Water Conservation Conference on Publicly Supplied Potable Water,* April 14–15, 1981, Denver, Colorado, National Bureau of Standards Special Publication No. 624, Gaithersburg, Maryland, June 1982.

Singell, Larry D., and Jane H. Lillydahl, "An Empirical Examination of the Effect of Impact Fees on the Housing Market," *Land Economics*, Vol. 66, No. 1, 1990, pp. 82–92.

Skaburskis, Andrej, and Mohammad Qadeer, "An Empirical Estimation of the Price Effects of Development Impact Fees," *Urban Studies*, Vol. 29, No. 5, 1992, pp. 653–667.

Skidmore, Mark, and Michael Peddle, "Do Development Impact Fees Reduce the Rate of Residential Development?" *Growth and Change*, Vol. 29, No. 4, 1998, pp. 383–393.

Soper, Spencer, "State Blasts County Water Conservation Efforts," *Santa Rosa Press Democrat*, November 19, 2004.

Speir, Cameron, and Kurt Stephenson, "Does Sprawl Cost Us All? Isolating the Effects of Housing Patterns on Public Water and Sewer Costs," *Journal of the American Planning Association*, Vol. 68, No. 1, Winter 2002, pp. 56–70.

Statewide Database, *Statewide Database*, 2000, available at http://swdb.berkeley.edu/info/PDRDocument.txt.

Tarlock, A. Dan, "The Future of Prior Appropriation in the New West," *Natural Resources Journal*, Vol. 41, Fall 2001, pp. 769–793.

Thomas, Gregory, *Designing Successful Groundwater Banking Programs in the Central Valley: Lessons from Experience*, Natural Heritage Institute, Berkeley, California, August 2001.

Vellinga, Mary Lynne, "Voters Set Stage for Growth in Three Areas" *Sacramento Bee*. November 4, 2004.

Waterman, Ryan, "Addressing California's Uncertain Water Future by Coordinating Long-Term Land-Use and Water Planning: Is a Water Element in the General Plan the Next Step?" *Ecology Law Quarterly*, Vol. 3, No. 1, 2004, pp.117–204.

Yinger, John, "The Incidence of Development Fees and Special Assessments," *National Tax Journal*, Vol. 51, No. 1, 1998, pp. 23–41.

About the Author

ELLEN HANAK

Ellen Hanak is a research fellow at the Public Policy Institute of California. Her career has focused on the economics of natural resource management and agricultural development. At PPIC, she has launched a research program on water policy. From 1992 to 2001, she was a research economist at the Center for Cooperation in International Agricultural Development (CIRAD), France, and before that held positions at the President's Council of Economic Advisers and the World Bank. She holds a B.A. in history from Swarthmore College, an M.A. in economics from the University of Dar es Salaam, Tanzania, and a Ph.D. in economics from the University of Maryland.

Related PPIC Publications

California 2025: Taking on the Future
Ellen Hanak and Mark Baldassare, editors

California's Infrastructure Policy for the 21st Century: Issues and Opportunities
David E. Dowall

Cities Under Pressure: Local Growth Controls and Residential Development Policy
Paul G. Lewis and Max Neiman

Making Room for the Future: Rebuilding California's Infrastructure
David E. Dowall and Jan Whittington

Metropolitan Growth Planning in California, 1900–2000
Elisa Barbour

Who Pays for Development Fees and Exactions?
Marla Dresch and Steven M. Sheffrin

Who Should Be Allowed to Sell Water in California? Third-Party Issues and the Water Market
Ellen Hanak

PPIC publications may be ordered by phone or from our website
(800) 232-5343 [mainland U.S.]
(415) 291-4400 [outside mainland U.S.]
www.ppic.org